T0292793

Quality Standards for Highly Effective Government

Second Edition

Quality Standards for Highly Effective Government

Second Edition

Richard E. Mallory

Routledge
Taylor & Francis Group
711 Third Avenue, New York, NY 10017

© 2018 by Taylor & Francis Group, LLC
Productivity Press is an imprint of Taylor & Francis Group, an Informa business

No claim to original U.S. Government works

Printed on acid-free paper

International Standard Book Number-13: 978-1-138-48239-5 (Hardback)
International Standard Book Number-13: 978-1-351-05799-8 (eBook)

Visit the Taylor & Francis Web site at
http://www.taylorandfrancis.com

and the Productivity Press site at
http://www.ProductivityPress.com

Contents

Acknowledgments

This book would not have come about but for the support and encouragement of my colleagues in the American Society for Quality Government Division, beginning with Past Chairs Dale Weeks and Bruce Waltuck, who encouraged us to develop "big audacious goals"; and Steve Wilson, of the National Oceanic and Atmospheric Administration, who has been continually there for support of our Division. I must also acknowledge Brian DeNiese, who encouraged me to serve as Government Division Chair in 2013 and 2014. I have also been thankful for the continuing support of past chairs and Government Division leadership including John Baranzelli, Mark Abrams, Marc Berson, Chris Shepherd, Mary 'Jo' Caldwell, Josh Smith, Bonnie Gaughan-Bailey, Janice Stout, and Mendy Richard, who have all been important friends and colleagues. Other friends and associates who have been important in this work include Fred Albert of the Federal Aviation Administration in Renton, Washington, and John Ward at Eastern Municipal Water District of Riverside County, California, who helped develop first versions of the process management standard.

Thanks also to my good friends Denzil Verardo of the California State Senate Cost Control Commission and Jerry Mairani, past President of the ASQ, who were kind enough to provide review and feedback on this work.

This book is dedicated to my sons Eric, Kevin, and Joe, and my daughter Julie—they demonstrate quality and love of life in everything they do—also to my wife, Cathy, a life-long source of love and inspiration.

Introduction: Transforming Government

This second edition of Auditable Quality Standards reflects a recognition that this book is establishing a "new normal" in government that will ultimately reinvent the practice of democratic government. The principal catalyst for this change will be the adoption of auditable quality standards within every government entity—based on efficiency, effectiveness, and delivered value. If you were to ask any person, or every person today, whether they believe that government is working well or is broken, it is a certainty that the big majority would say it is broken. Conventional wisdom says that government is *not* efficient and *not* effective, that it is missing a big dose of common sense, and that it costs too much. But truth be told, no one really knows what works and what is broken in government, where to find some common sense, and where to start to fix it.

The problem sounds huge, but the solution is not all that difficult. Quality science* *can* provide a structure for efficiency and effectiveness, democratic institutions *can* create consensus goals, and auditable standards *can* show where these things exist and to what degree. It can also drive change where it needs to happen, because if you can measure it, you can manage it.[†] Auditable quality standards have the potential to make these unknowns highly visible, and to offer a clear scorecard that anyone can follow. They can provide holistic and thorough measurements because they will align with the unique roles and responsibilities at three fundamental levels of leadership in government. The three levels are these: (1) work unit supervisors and managers at the "front line" of government service; (2) chief executives, department directors, and their deputies as "Executive Management" of government agencies, and (3) elected leadership at the top, as those key officials that must define the priorities, outcomes, programs, and budgets.

---

* The term "quality science" will be defined in Chapter 2, and refers to the tools and knowledge associated with quality management. It has its origins beginning in the Toyota Production System of the 1970s, and embraces a broad body of professional knowledge about doing things right the first time. It is the basis of the U.S. National Quality Award and the Japanese Deming Prize.
† It is often said that if you cannot measure it, you cannot manage it. The premise of this book is that the efficiency and effectiveness of government today is not easily measurable. It is the purpose of auditable standards to change that.

There are three parts to the auditable standards that align with the three levels of leadership. They include the following:

1. Process management standards: That align with the public-facing work processes at the level of the front-line supervisor.
2. Structured systems management standards: That provide a framework for evaluating the management of overall organizational systems and apply at the Executive Level.
3. Aligned leadership objectives: That uncover whether elected officials have agreed on prioritized outcomes and objectives for government, and whether they are individually rewarded for or held accountable for results.

The process management standard aligns with the front-line managers and supervisors in government, who manage the front-line workers that look the public in the eye. The structured systems management standard will hold mid- and executive-level managers accountable for the higher-level frameworks and systems the link processes end-to-end, and that provide a scorecard for overall agency and department performance. The standards for aligned leadership objectives will hold elected leaders accountable for agreeing on prioritized goals for each agency and department, and for providing a scorecard for the public on how well *they* are doing, as the public's "board of directors."

The auditable quality standards are essential because government, by its nature, *should* contribute to the long-term value of society and human civilization, and the auditable standards will provide a focus on the long-term that does not exist today. Presently, neither elected leaders nor executive leadership in government is rewarded or recognized for long-term results. Both push hard for immediate and short-term results because they are easier to achieve, and focused on by a public that has nothing else to judge. So, an elected official that "fires" a city manager who is slow to repair roads is seen to have "done something," while the former City Manager who was trying to marshal resources for a major highway improvement program (instead of "fixing potholes") is judged to have "done nothing."

Upwardly mobile government managers and elected officials share the desire to show quick results, so they can move on to their next, and higher level, job. Neither intends to be around when long-term results crash, so they can let the next guy worry about that, and the public is none the wiser. The system as it exists has very little motivation or reward for those in government who seek real value or the long-term benefit. The dis-alignment comes from the fact that our public-sector management systems and our elected democratic leadership continue to be motivated by short-term appearances, since there are no recognized measures of social value nor of whether government is stronger tomorrow than it was today.* In a system where no one must report on results, no one can be held accountable. But that can change!

The transformation of government envisioned by this book will come about when the annual financial audit required in every local, state, and federal government is accompanied by a Certified Public Quality Audit using the standards introduced here. Alternately, the governments themselves may choose to use the standards internally and to certify the quality of all the major work flows they perform. In this way they can be sure that all managers are using the well-known and proven techniques of Lean and Continuous Quality Improvement and achieving the greatest possible benefit for the public.

The *only* thing that stands in the way of the future achievement is an understanding that the use of quality practices is not difficult or abstract, and that measurement of the capability and maturity of work is possible, and useful. This book provides the standard of practice on which such efforts can be established, and from which they can grow.

The three levels of audit proposed are critical because all three levels must work together, or the work of the others will be compromised. Perhaps the general public is only vaguely aware that the failure of elected representatives to be able to agree on goals is having a devastating impact on the efficiency of government at lower levels, but a direct relationship exists. The coordinated work of all three levels is essential to create best value at lowest cost, and one level will always be impaired by a failure of the other two. All three auditable standards must be embraced to ensure best value at lowest cost for our greater society.

Specifically, it is the work of front-line supervisors and managers to ensure the efficiency and effectiveness of individual government processes. Efficiency is typically defined as the ability to obtain greater or better outputs at lower or equal resource costs. Effectiveness is typically defined as the ability of the process to consistently produce the value that is desired, with the lowest possible waste and required rework of things not done

---

* It can be argued that a unique role of government is to focus on long term and to correct an intrinsic bias of individual citizens and private enterprise to focus on short-term goals at the detriment of the longer-term interests of society. Pollution control is an example of this. However, where the government does not accept its role to focus on the long term, who will?

right the first time. And while it is pretty clear that a front-line manager is responsible for developing and maintaining efficient and effective processes within their own span of control, those can easily break down if there is a failure to provide them with critical resources.* So, for example, it is apparent that even the best front-line process will languish and fail if the supervisor cannot hire and train key personnel. Since it is the responsibility of senior and executive management to make sure that processes are supported and coordinated, it suddenly becomes apparent that both the front-line and executive management of an agency must both be "on their game" if the intended end result is to be achieved.

In the same way, the value created by the portfolio of processes within any agency depends on the second and third levels—and it can only come about through the coordinated work of both the executive management and the elected representatives. This is true because when any agency is rapidly asked to change its goals or priorities, loses necessary support or authority, or is asked to undertake more programs and initiatives than it can handle within its existing resource base, it will need to deliberately sub-optimize one existing process or activity, to accommodate another. So, for example, if a legislative body undertakes unnecessary "oversight hearings" because of an unpreventable accident, its senior managers and their direct reports will need to suspend planned work to provide analysis and answers. Or if an outcome of those hearings is to double check every future agency action to prevent error, the resources devoted to unnecessary double-checking will need to be removed from primary and planned activities.

In effect, either deliberately or accidentally, the interchange between elected leaders and the executive management of each agency defines what it is important to do—the *value* that the organization must achieve. If there is a "fuzzy" or conflicted values statement, then none of the defined values can be achieved well since there is no way to budget for unknown or unclear requirements.

The only management reality is that the standardization and control of key systems are necessary for sustained, long-term efficiency and effectiveness—and value. Based on this premise, this book introduces the concept of defined *value* as a precondition for efficiency and effectiveness and presents the theory that the fundamental failure of government to

---

* There are other factors of executive management that can either impair or improve front-line processes, such as its willingness to assist in removing barriers to efficient and effective work. Those will be discussed in a later chapter.

routinely achieve efficiency and effectiveness is due to the failure of our elected leaders and the executive management of government agencies to define value, and to work together to achieve value. This will be the focus of the third audit standard—aligned systems objectives.

As a result, this book proposes that a focus on efficiency and effectiveness, combined with its defined value, provides the foundation of effective government and of its audit standard. Since the *value* to be created is the purpose of any government agency, and *efficiency* and *effectiveness* are the way the services should be delivered, we can call this sought-after foundation VEE, or more simply VE-2.

This book also provides four necessary strategies that will support the use of these standards including:

1. Create an imperative for consensus
2. End incentives for building bureaucracy
3. Build a safety net for champions of efficiency
4. Make elected representatives accountable for results

This book presents the methods necessary to measure and improve the quality of organizational systems in government, across the board, and on a sustained basis to achieve value, efficiency, and effectiveness (VE-2). It is a manifesto for the government of the future which provides a map to the future and which will be of benefit to us all.

Author

Richard E. Mallory is an acknowledged expert on government, having served for three years as a professional staff member for a U.S. Senator, nine years as a senior executive in both state and federal government, and for over 20 years as a consultant to federal, state, and local governments. His exceptional knowledge of government operations comes from service as an advisor to hundreds of jurisdictions and agencies around the United States, as the Director of the California Department of Housing and Community Development, and as California–Nevada State Director for the U.S. Department of Agriculture. Mallory is a seven-time Examiner for the Baldrige Quality Award, six times for the California State Award, and once at the national level. Currently he is a senior project manager for CPS HR Consulting and chair of Government Division of the American Society for Quality. Mallory is the author of three books on quality in government and is an experienced presenter on the subject. He holds a Master's Degree in management and is a Certified Project Management Professional.

1

The Problem and the Promise

Government is unique in that the economic reality that confronts almost every other kind of economic entity does not confront government—it will never go out of business because of a lack of delivered quality* or competition. The problem is that there is no "invisible hand" that guides government services naturally to meet the demands of its customers. Only elected representatives are available to shutter those that do not work, and the record of such shut-downs is almost non-existent. Something new is required, and the Auditable Standards for Highly Effective Government are that solution.

Municipal bankruptcy notwithstanding, there is not one poorly operated city (or more specifically a municipal corporation) that will be closed and cease to exist. When cities are so badly managed that they cannot pay all their bills, a court may appoint a receiver to remove the discretionary powers of the city council or to restructure its operations, but the city structure will remain in some form, as if it has eternal life. The taxpayers will be required to continue to pay for its operations through taxes. Government must provide essential public services and it must ensure that public obligations are met.

Even though government must continue to operate, its efficiency is always in question because its revenue stream, through taxes, is automatically collected each year on a formula basis. It does not depend on individual taxpayers agreeing to "buy" a set of government services for the year, and those taxpayers do not have a choice of providers. It is structured as a monopoly to a captive consumer base. It is the pre-eminent bundled package of services.

---

* This book uses the word "quality" as a defined term, as noted in the second chapter. It is based on the science of "continuous quality improvement" and structured process improvement.

Part of the difficulty of effectively managing government comes from the fact that there is no direct line from someone who wants a specific type of products and services, to the agency or office that provides that type of products and services, and with a series of individual transactions* showing that the services were or were not effectively and efficiently provided to the persons or entities who wanted those services to begin with. Government is missing the most important input for the practice of "quality science"—it is missing the Voice of the Customer. There is no one direct "customer" of government services that determines the value of what is received—nor could there be.

In the first place, the concept of equity in government means that fairness and other attributes of public purpose enter into each transaction. So, for example, in matters of justice, or giving various kinds of monetary support, corollary issues serving other purposes are as important as the transaction initially desired by a distinct individual. In addition, even individual agencies perform multiple services, so a description of what each agency does, for whom, and to what effect or outcome, is arguable.

Unlike private business, citizens and taxpayers cannot input a marketplace decision about the individual services they want or receive—taxes are "automatically" levied on behalf of the group of departments and offices that are included within the jurisdiction. In addition, the division of taxes between the various agencies that spend the money is also by formula—through legislative and budgeting action—and none of the individual agencies depend on a positive marketplace decision—they each get a legislatively determined "piece of the pie." There is no self-correcting economic motivation as there would be for the divisions of a single company that would show the products and services of one division were very widely accepted by consumers while those of another were suffering. Government is a package deal, with funding provided through an annual budget, and there is no "invisible hand" that encourages agencies to grow and improve in the areas of customer satisfaction, or efficiency. It sounds like a hopeless mess, that will never sort itself out, but it does not have to be.

Some may argue that those who hold political office must serve in the place of customers, as primary stakeholders, and that through their collective political actions they must provide the correct economic motivation and leadership direction for quality to result. However, while having

---

* In the private sector these would be cash transactions—purchase decisions.

legislators as surrogate customers might work in theory, the actual experience has been different. Our elected leaders are not at all like corporate directors in that they do not have a vested interest in the *overall* positive performance of the governments for whom they are supposedly "accountable." Their most direct line of responsibility is to the small group of special interests on which they depend for the preponderance of their campaign re-election funding, and secondarily to the members of the majority political party within the geographic area in which they are elected—which could be as little as one-third to one-fourth of the total adult population in that district. Within some reasonable bounds of behavior, a long tenure in office can often be achieved by any politician who can deliver only those votes that are viewed favorably by his or her special interest supporters, through obtaining "key" partisan votes and through obtaining a generous amount of funding for local projects.

A further problem is that elected officials do not get good information to know where to cut even if they have the highest and most noble public interests. For example, how can your Congressman determine whether the Federal Department of Education is doing as good a job as the Department of Housing and Urban Development, or if either or both are unnecessary or in need of improvement? Or how would Congress get early warning that three of the major programs within the Departments are very poorly run, while the remainder are doing exemplary work?*

Lately it has been observed that the major political parties fail to assume responsibility for reaching consensus decisions and even restrain their members from discussing consensus solutions unless they are shared in by party leadership. This has resulted in leaving government in the chaos of "no decision," due to the inability to reach agreement.† This latest phenomenon is also quite dissimilar from the management of private business, where corporate directors would be dismissed or sued if they did not make necessary decisions to ensure the appropriate functioning of their organization.

---

* It is noted that the U.S. federal government does have an Office of the Inspector General that does periodic agency audits, and many state and local entities have similar kinds of audit offices that perform similar reviews. But these reviews are conducted on a random basis, are often focused on a single program or process, and do not provide comprehensive and prospective indicators of problems.

† Obvious recent examples include the U.S. Congress failing to enact many annual budgets, debt ceiling increases, and deficit reduction agreements. Many states have also seen multiple examples of similar behavior by their legislatures. The need to create an imperative for consensus building in government is discussed further in Chapter 8.

Corporate directors realize that they cannot always "get their way" and refuse to agree to any other approach to make a necessary decision. They cannot allow the corporation for which they are responsible perish for lack of direction. Congressmen, however, in our present partisan democracy, are not held to this standard.

It is also impossible to rely solely on the hired civil servants and their management teams to independently implement an efficient and effective government structure. Government workers and managers are constrained because of their understandable desire for a stable and secure job with an opportunity to advance and grow their career in the future. Government managers who point out that their programs (or even singular components of programs) are not good value can often draw strong attack from the special interests who put the programs there in the first place, and who can influence their key legislative supporters to trade votes with colleagues to keep them in place. At the same time, such managers can lose support of their own workforce, who see their own jobs being threatened and who now see their senior managers as "dis-loyal" to the organization. Lastly, managers who take action to reduce the size of their organization can activate fear among their own managers and supervisors, who can see that if the size of their workforce is diminished, or the number of program offices reduced, that the "complexity" and "scope" of their own civil service job classifications could be reduced, and their positions could be downgraded or eliminated.* This would be the equivalent of willingly working for your own demotion or termination.

This previous discussion is the root cause of the continuing failure to find a way to cut waste from government without resorting to across-the-board cuts. Even though it is widely agreed that when there is "fat in government" it should be removed precisely within the pockets and veins where it exists, and without resort to a "meat axe," that almost never happens. It almost never happens because those who know where fat exists have absolutely no incentive to report it. They also have a great deal of fear about coming forward with that information. The recommendations in this book will change that!

At the same time, the voting public only sees the end result of their mismanaged government, a series of sub-optimized systems that seem perennially unable to achieve efficiency, effectiveness, and common sense. There

---

* This point is discussed further in Chapter 8, under the heading, "End Incentives for Building Bureaucracy."

is no way to insist on quality management in government, or to remove elected officials who do not achieve quality, **when its presence is invisible**.

The primary purpose of these Auditable Standards for Government is to **make the presence of quality in government measurable and auditable**, so the existence of competent management in government branches, programs, bureaus, and departments is completely transparent. These guidelines make this possible through an objective, defined, and auditable process certification guideline, as its base.

Because key processes are fundamental to every office and bureau, no matter how small, this auditable process management standard makes it possible for each manager and supervisor to develop a report card on their management practice. Uniform audits using the standard can be performed across all types of government, and at all levels.

A classic management book of the past identified a fundamental problem of meetings called to discuss public sector issues that it called "the multi-headed animal syndrome."* It was described as a tendency of groups gathered for discussion of a single issue to "go off in all directions at once," so that the participants even forget why they first gathered. A political discourse suffering from the multi-headed animal syndrome can easily proceed from a single initial issue—such as whether to establish a cross walk at a particular location—to a variety of surrounding matters, such as speed limits, whether police adequately patrol the area, whether the city can afford it, and who might be hired to do the work. Without an agreed-upon purpose for a meeting, any solution will do, and the debate can go in circles for hours without anything being done.

This explains why the past discussions of cutting waste in government go in circles. It is because there is no shared agenda on which to base discussion, and there is no objective standard supporting a review. Implementation of an auditable standard will provide a beginning point for change because it will (ultimately) provide an agreed-upon list of priorities for that government jurisdiction, a scorecard to show how well each priority is addressed, and an efficiency and effectiveness score for each agency charged with accomplishment of that scorecard. With this information, the areas for action will be clear. It will then allow hired public-sector managers to apply proven methods of quality science and

---

* *How to Make Meetings Work*, by Michael Doyle and David Straus, Jove Books, New York, Sept. 1982. Page 20.

process management to deliver value and achieve the intended purpose of government.*

The book is intended to provide a means for government at all levels to focus on what is most important, and to provide value, efficiency and effectiveness in what our government agrees to provide. Society is currently witness to a clash of parties and institutions on a broad scale, that has spawned a chaotic mélange of criticism, litigation, and advocacy that trumps leadership and spurns good management in many ways—the multi-headed animal syndrome. It threatens the core of the good that is at the heart of our democracy. It is the Christmas present and Christmas future of our nation unless something is done about it, and this book will map the "something" that is needed.

It must be recognized that many political advocates see the solution to our current problem as the elimination of government. And while there are valid reasons to limit the overall spending on the public sector, it is acknowledged that government brings a unique value to society that no other entity can provide. For example, we would all suffocate in pollution but for the agency of government.

However, the focus on unleashing the potential value of our government is being lost. It would seem that the debate over limiting government has been much more successful at diverting the public attention away from obtaining best value from government, and much more successful on attacking its apparent cost, and some specific programs. In many circles people are only interested in discussing what government should not do, rather than what it can do or what it is there to accomplish.

The necessity of government was perhaps best described by Abraham Lincoln when he said that government exists to do those essential works that no one man can do, or will do, for himself. While those who attack government generally favor what they might call "natural rights," it is in fact government that defines and protects those natural rights within groups of people that might not be inclined to do so. Government protects our right to property, both through maintaining property titles, and defending claims against those who would prevent or impair our use of property through the courts, and through the enforcement of court orders by the local police department! Clearly, government is an enabler and a partner to our private sector, and not a competitor for its resources.

---

* Further discussed in Chapter 10.

With that said, those who can only complain about the high tax rates we pay should instead ask themselves if they would rather live and operate a business in the Congo or Somalia, where tax rates, along with personal security, social services, and opportunity, are much lower.

The singular vision of this book is the implementation of a uniform auditable standard of quality in government. It offers a framework for a day in the not-too-distant future when a quality audit can provide a uniform and valid "benchmark" report card on every government agency in America that is a companion to the annual audit of the financial books. The quality audit will be a report card that spans the *two sides of government*—with scores relevant to the hired government workers and their management team, *and* a score for the elected leadership that sits as its public "board of directors."

Auditable Standards for Government are envisioned as a first step in a fundamental reshaping of the American system of governance that will eliminate its bloat and lethargy and make it a fit and productive partner for our entrepreneurial society in the next century. Auditable Standards will provide for reform of the American system of governance in several fundamental ways: First, it provides for an independent and objective evaluation of the efficiency and effectiveness of government at any level, that will inform and provide the basis for action when deficiencies are discovered. Second, it recognizes that government is a system made up of elected leaders on the one side and hired workers and managers on the other, and that the fundamental *value* of government—what it achieves—can only be controlled by elected leaders.

It introduces the idea of value as the fundamental driver for efficiency and effectiveness. Every government agency everywhere has limited manpower, and cannot undertake to do everything well. They cannot continue to change course as elected leaders add goals and requirements and modify budgets. The value of government depends on a focused set of goals, and a prioritized list of things it is asked to work on, and a consistency in maintaining that for a period of time.

Elected leaders represent the Board of Directors for all Americans. They should perform like the board of directors of any corporation, and must agree on priorities, set goals, and track progress. This elected board also needs to work with the government agency chief executive officer (or "CEO")—be that the President, Governor, Department Director, or City Manager—to eliminate constraints and barriers, balance the budget, and pay the bills. Their reward (pay and bonus) should be based on performance. Quite obviously this is not now being done, and either the pubic does not know how to make this happen or they have forgotten that this is the standard to which our elected leaders should be held accountable. The standard will offer means for both.

It is a major deficiency of most bipartisan political democracy that no one takes responsibility for the value created, and most political leaders maintain their reputation only by placing blame for the perceived failures of others. Peter Block* once equated partisan politics to an arena sport, where Republicans and Democrats come to the arena to cheer for their team to win, and no one takes responsibility for getting things done. They only care if they win or lose. This analogy of arena sports has been successfully grafted into our culture, with our premier news reporters gleefully speculating whether red states will ever turn blue, or vice versa. The story of government leadership is reported in the same terms as professional sports, or gang warfare. Our fifth estate should be clear about that fact that *nothing* is accomplished in government when the political parties fight a win-lose battle, and that value for the public is only created when there is collaboration and consensus.

As things stand there is no reward for elected representatives to define or resolve public problems—like the high cost of health care. It is easier to name and attack the other party's solution—"Obamacare," for example— and then bitterly attack its perceived flaws rather than offering a solution of your own or working together for a solution that both parties can support. The end game of win-lose politics is that one of the two sides "wins" with a partial solution at best, while the public loses since the entire problem (the high cost of health care) has not been fully identified or fully addressed. The highly charged win-lose environment also aids partisan leaders in rejecting responsibility for the flawed results because they never got all they wanted and can then always point to flaws that are the cause of future problems. It fosters an environment where elected leaders prefer not to work toward shared solutions because they will always have the ability to walk away from any future issues or problems. *They* are not responsible.

In the same way, once partisan leaders "win" (or lose), there is very limited further advantage for those officials to want to work with government agency executives to remove barriers and constraints in implementing the

---

* A recognized organizational development consultant and writer, perhaps best known as the author of the 1993 best-seller, *Stewardship: Choosing Service Over Self Interest*, and the 1991 book, *The Empowered Manager: Positive Political Skills at Work*.

program. It is far more beneficial to attack government when issues or mistakes arise because taking responsibility for programs raises the possibility of blame. However, government executives need the help of elected officials to eliminate barriers and resolve issues, since they often require either changes in law or changes in budgets to resolve problems. They need a partnership with elected officials to make programs work, and yet elected officials are often constrained in wanting to do so.

This book poses the proposition that the efficiency and effectiveness of government agencies depends on elected leaders sharing responsibility and working collaboratively, and that their failure to do so may be the largest reason that efficiency and effectiveness is not achieved. It advances the idea that government as a whole must be judged by its *defined value*, which is a result of agreement on goals and a shared scorecard, and that the level to which this is done can be an auditable standard. Even if the reporting of those audit results does not positively influence who is elected to office, this book proposes that legislators be denied the right to run for re-election if their agencies' performance does not achieve a minimum audit score. In this way there will be distinct incentives for elected officials to work together in the future, and to assume responsibility for results.

While it is possible to systematically evaluate the efficiency and effectiveness of government agencies as they are currently defined, this book introduces an auditable standard that is both uniform and objective, and which can show positive and negative changes over time. The need for a uniform auditable standard of quality in government is perhaps obvious, since without one there is no easy way to evaluate whether government is too large or too small, and whether any office or agency is working well, or is working poorly. As an entity with the power to tax, government does not face the primary constraint of every business enterprise to "make a profit." It therefore has no bottom line indicator of its performance. Likewise, government has a fatal flaw in the structure of its "board of directors"—our elected representatives—who are in fact its elected leadership.

The challenge is huge, but the need for change is apparent. The future depends on the transformation of government, and this includes our expectations for elected leadership. These new standards can ensure that: Each office, agency, or level of government has consensus goals and objectives, with priorities and measurable performance levels; the goals and objectives selected match the purpose of the government entity and public expectations for its operation; this scorecard is maintained and reviewed annually and is used as a report card for the voting public.

2

Quality as a Backbone

In the simplest terms, quality is a measure of delivered value, and when all is said and done, that is what citizens want from government. Most persons see taxes as painful but necessary, just the same as a utility bill, and they want to know their payments are not being wasted. Quality management speaks that language, and helps to document and show what you are getting, the cost of what you are getting, and possible areas for improvement.

The quality profession is a management science that seeks to ensure that the value achieved in any economic transaction is reliable and predictable. In other words, that if you purchase a new mobile telephone, the likelihood of its failure is very small.

The premiere organization promoting quality practice is the American Society for Quality (ASQ), which is now an international organization. It was established in 1946 to share knowledge and continue the use of analytic tools and quality-improvement techniques that had been developed to provide reliable ships, vehicles, and munitions during wartime. Form follows function and it makes sense that during the war the armed services wanted industry to provide munitions and delivery systems with the highest possible reliability, more than they wanted the lowest cost per unit. Quality systems blossomed in that environment, and the ASQ was founded to maintain and advance those systems, while American industry was shifting back to mass production at lowest cost.

While post-war American producers slowly deserted quality and swung back to lowest cost production, they found growing competition in the 1970s from Japan and Germany, whose automotive industries had both recovered and embraced quality as their foundational practice. By the 1980s quality was recognized everywhere as an imperative, as Japanese electronics and computer manufacturers were able to provide both high reliability and lowest cost.

The principles of quality practice were also evolving, and ASQ members began to see that ensuring the value of organizational outputs required attention to standardized best practices in production processes, but also in systems such as the selection and training of personnel. Ensuring quality could come about by eliminating the root causes of waste, but more importantly by building reliable processes and systems that prevented problems and focused on "error-proofing."

The current practice of quality in business requires a focus on customers and value to define the requirements (or desired performance metrics) of what is being produced, and it applies a scientific method to analysis of what could be improved, and methods of improving it. Currently popular applications of quality in the private sector include Lean Process Management, Six Sigma, Kaizen, ISO process certification, and some others—all of which are forms of Continuous Quality Improvement—or more simply, "quality science."

Quality science is the study of people engaged in work that creates a beneficial thing (value) for a user (customer) through a work flow that is efficient and effective. That work flow should also be reliable and consistent (no variation) and continually improving. It uses a scientific method of observation, hypothesis, testing, evaluation, and implementation, with a reliance on data. Quality management has now been successfully proven in service and manufacturing, and is an established practice in many organizations because it provides the underpinning of customer satisfaction and profitability.* It has been an engine for tremendous gains in the reliability of products, and in driving down their costs, since the late 1980s.

The practice of quality is at odds with the mass marketing approach that attempts to create consumer demand for products and services through advertising and limited markets (like cell phone service under contract) and then seeks to provide the product or service at low cost and without regard to its reliability, or the length of time it will be in service.

There are many important foundational practices that are important to quality, and indeed a quality science has come about that has carried forward those practices, so that the development of efficiency and effectiveness in processes, and specifically in government processes, is not really a mystery. The practice of quality science has been preserved and fostered

---

* The antithesis of quality practice is a focus on short-term results, which can often boost profits temporarily, but will always result in the return of error and waste, and lost customer loyalty.

by the American Society for Quality, which itself has grown to be a global organization with members in more than 140 countries.

Through the structured use of quality science—a focus on process management, continuous improvement, and structured problem solving—government leaders anywhere *could* have the highest levels of efficiency and effectiveness. The problem lies in the fact that elected political leadership is not motivated to want efficiency and effectiveness. Elected leaders are more closely aligned with the cited mass market approach, and are more motivated to fight for the least cost of all government programs, instead of best value services. This is the reason that Auditable Standard of Quality in government is essential, and that implementation of an auditable standard can make a huge difference in the value and efficiency of government services because it can make it apparent where quality exists and where it is lacking.

One of the fundamental rules of management is that if it can't be measured, it can't be managed. Since objective measures drive what is seen, acknowledged, and discussed, it makes sense that things that can't be seen or measured won't be part of the discussion. Because there is now no objective way to measure the efficiency and effectiveness of government agencies, elected representatives can only look at what is measurable—its cost. Auditable Standards for Highly Effective Government will change that. The vision of this book is to create that accountability through an auditable standard that supports systematic use of quality science.

3

The Process Management Standard and the Unifying Theory of Work

The foundational components of work process analysis

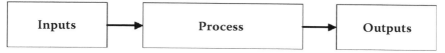

Quality in government is provided through efficient and effective delivery of goods and services that meet end user requirements, and it is the unit manager's job to ensure that the resources entrusted to them obtain that intended result. Management textbooks tell us that this must be done through the activities of planning, organizing, controlling, supervising, directing, and training. This activity is thought to be directed at the "work" and the "worker," in a variety of ways. While true, the *most* important role is that of shaping and controlling work activity of individuals through process management. This *should* be the primary focus of managers in government, but it is mostly overlooked and ignored because many managers get lost in looking at the detail of individual people and tasks, the volume or the variation of those tasks, and responding to incidental and political issues.

Many managers get stuck in looking at people and events because it is our human nature to want to judge people good and bad, stars and laggers, and to blame *them* for any bad thing that happens. It is also acknowledged that many managers like to be "fire fighters," and jump in at the time of big problems so they can find the workers that made mistakes and be acknowledged for making things better. This is a comfortable role for some managers because they are perceived as being removed from the problems and associated with the solutions. However, if we expand our expectation for government managers to say that part of their job is to select good people and train them properly and to set up processes that will rarely fail, then the problems that occur are not the responsibility of workers, but of managers.

It is this proactive perspective that leads us to the conclusion that process management is the primary role of work unit managers and supervisors. Indeed, process management is a critical management job and can only be done by a manager or supervisor. No individual worker can do that job by themselves. Process management holds managers responsible for making every worker a winner. It is a much higher standard, but has been proven to be the correct one.

There is a famous television comedy skit from the renowned "I Love Lucy" series in which Lucille Ball and her friend, Ethel Mertz, are hired at a candy factory, and asked to wrap chocolate candies as they come down a conveyor belt, and to place the wrapped candies back on the belt for packaging. The goal is to wrap each candy and to avoid having any unwrapped candies move to the next station. The belt first runs too slowly and then too quickly, and soon they are performing hilarious work adaptations (like eating the chocolates and putting them in their pockets) to avoid being fired. While funny to watch, managers who focus only on workers and outputs rather than on the process are equally negligent, and not at all funny. These managers are looking at the things they have least ability to control (work inputs, individual actions, and output) rather than the one thing they *can* control—the process! This kind of behavior puts its focus on "non-standard" performance rather than on helping workers to do the right thing right the first time, through training, work process set up, and work process support. Managers who support process spend their time in preparing work and workers to do quality work and establishing processes that either greatly reduce or eliminate the possibility of error.

It is the theory of this book that the general angst expressed about a lack of efficiency and effectiveness in government is in large measure due to the failure of government managers and supervisors to manage their processes. Beginning with the time of the publication of this book, this is an unforgivable and entirely avoidable omission in which elected leaders are complicit, because they can now *require* process management and audit to ensure that it is in place.

Both this chapter and the succeeding chapter are based on a *unifying theory of work management* that is new to quality science, and since that unifying theory is necessary to a full and complete understanding of what is being offered, this chapter begins with a short history and explanation.

One of the founders of quality science, W. Edwards Deming, introduced his work with a description of a "system," and in that discussion, he provided a set of fundamental principles that apply both to "process" as described in this chapter, and "system" as defined in the next. Deming defines a human system as "a network of interdependent components that work together to accomplish the aim of the system."* Not surprisingly, he also says that, "A system must have an aim.† Without an aim, there is no system." Those observations are also completely true of a process.

In short, Dr. Deming envisions a system (or process) as a collection of resources under the span of control of a leader. The resources given to a manager are the people, computers and information resources, machines and equipment, authorities, and established business systems. As Steven Covey argues, every person (and certainly every manager) has a set of things under their direct control and under their indirect influence.‡ This is the resource base envisioned by Dr. Deming that defines his or her "system." In this framework, the "aim" is the business purpose for this manager, and the reason that the resources are made available. The "aim" is the same as that manager's program purpose or goals. It is also the yardstick by which its value should be reviewed. In that context, the leader's ability to achieve that aim or to improve on previous results is the highest value.

Stopping briefly to focus on the observations of Dr. Deming, we might ask how many government managers have clearly defined an "aim" or business purpose for their key processes, and have a demonstrated ability to deliver consistently and/or to improve their business result? This is the challenge of process management.

Taking this concept just a bit further, we can look at the nature of *all* the work of government. The *unifying theory of work management* states that all work has some repetitive factors, and that managers can learn from past experience and constructively apply that learning to the future so that better results, or improvement, can take place. The ability to learn from the past is highest when the work has repetitive features, particularly in what it seeks to accomplish and where there is an expectation for similar results. It also helps where the people, methods, and resources are familiar

---

* W. Edwards Deming, *The New Economics*, Massachusetts Institute of Technology, Center for Advanced Engineering Study, 1993. pp. 50–51.
† The word "aim" is synonymous with "purpose," and suggests that delivered value is the aim of government systems and processes.
‡ Steven R. Covey (1989). *The Seven Habits of Highly Effective People*, pp. 81–88. Simon and Schuster, New York.

to the organization and easily available. This, indeed, is the definition of a process, and its features can be summarized as:

1. Work that has commonality of steps and resources, and
2. Work that has commonality in its resource group.

This kind of work is best managed using the "tool" of process management because it will benefit from standard, "best practice" methods, will provide "lessons learned," will be subject to continuous improvement, and will respond positively to the *scientific method*. This chapter introduces the process management standard* as a basic blueprint for process management in government, and the process certification criteria as a way of objectively measuring the maturity of processes, and its relative level of efficiency and effectiveness. In other words, it presents an objective means of evaluating whether any manager and process is gaining maximum benefit from the scientific method, or alternately, is allowing sloppy work instead.

Looking again at the manager's duties, it's pretty clear that the only "platform" for their planning, organizing, and controlling activity is the series of repetitive tasks that shape the primary work output for their work unit and training or coaching the workers so they can do their part. The series of tasks *is a process.*[†] Process is generally defined as: A set of defined incremental activities that transform an input to a valuable output for an end-user or customer. Process then, is the "atomic particle" of work unit management, and the act of standardizing that process to get a uniform output is a basic activity of process management. If managers do a good job at process management and incorporate continuous improvements, they might be able to argue they have achieved "best practice."

The following process management standard has been adopted by the American Society for Quality Government Division,[‡] and provides an objective method for evaluating whether any government manager or

---

* The process management standard, the system management standard, and the aligned leadership objective standards presented in this book have been adopted and endorsed by the Government Division of the American Society for Quality as international best practices. The versions of each presented are those most recently updated, but the reader may also want to download current versions from www.asq.org/gov.

† Work is done through projects, process, and activity, but most is done through process.

‡ The author created this standard for government primarily based on the previous work of Cherian Varghese, CCE, in his paper, *Resolving the Process Paradox: A Strategy for Launching Meaningful Business Process Improvement*, published in Cost Engineering, Volume 46, Number 11, November 2004. He also gives thanks to his professional colleagues within the Leadership Council of Government Division.

supervisor is practicing process management and continuous improvement, and the level of discipline or accomplishment that has been applied. It provides for three fundamental areas of evaluation, including:

1. The definition and documentation of a standard process that is believed to be best practice.
2. The definition and use of at least one key process measure that is based on known customer requirements and process design requirements.
3. A record of process improvement and employee involvement in process improvement.

Each criterion has multiple defined levels of maturity as noted in Table 3.1, and the balance of this chapter will provide discussion of the logic behind each criterion, and their associated levels of maturity.

Organizations using this model for process certification are asked to require each manager and supervisor to identify at least one key process within their span of control. A common method of doing so would be through development of a "SIPOC" diagram, in which the manager lists all the suppliers, inputs, processes, output, and customers (those who use outputs) of their program office.* Each designated process must then define its beginning and end point, with a defined and documented outcome. To ensure accuracy, each process should be rated by independent observers or existing audit staff in each of the three process maturity criteria. A very mature process could score 15 points in this matrix, while one that was not standardized would score zero.

The process management standard is provided as an "open source" model of certifying the maturity (or capability) of process management in any government office. Its primary benefit is that it can rapidly be put in use by government agencies with very little up-front investment and without extensive training. It supports two fundamental rules of good management: First, if you can't measure it, you can't manage it. Second, good management structure requires that those accountable for resources be held responsible for showing results at the lowest possible level.

Appropriate use of the model is also based on a fundamental belief of quality science, that management must take ownership for 85%–95% of problems discovered and should not try to blame employees. When problems are discovered, they should be "owned" by all of management, until a

---

* A SIPOC diagram and instructions for using it are provided in the appendix of this book.

TABLE 3.1

Process Management Standard

Standard Process	Measurements	Process Improvement/Employee Empowerment
0 – Process is not standardized.	0 – Customer and process design requirements are unknown.	0 – No systematic improvement efforts. No employee involvement.
1 – A process flowchart or procedure document exists but may not be current or complete.	1 – Some customer/process design requirements have been established but are often based on dissatisfaction, waste, or error.	1 – A few process improvements all based on management initiatives.
2 – Process flowchart or procedure document exists and is current/complete.	2 – Customer/process design requirements have been established and validated and exist at an auditable level.	2 – A few process improvements based on employee suggestions.
3 – Process flow is regularly updated. Aim is clear and periodic feedback is obtained.	3 – Several key process measures exist, and at least one is a leading in-process measure. Results are regularly reviewed by management.	3 – A fact-based structure for analysis and problem solving is in place.
4 – Flowchart or procedure document is regularly referenced and is used for training. Regular feedback is provided.	4 – Several key process measures exist, representing supplier inputs, in-process measures, outputs, and outcomes. Measures are validated against customer and design requirements, and updated based on learning.	4 – The workforce participates in continuous improvement and it follows an established problem solving structure—*tools are used.*
5 – Flowchart is uniformly used at an auditable standard. It is linked to metrics and continuous improvement efforts.	5 – Process measures show the process is stable and performing within control limits. Measures are linked to competitive comparisons or benchmark organizations.	5 – There is evidence of continuous systematic improvement and measurable, positive results.

root cause is determined and a best solution is devised. Putting blame for poor work performance on any one individual misses the point. Process improvement requires that all parties assist in development and implementation of its solution.*

The power of this process management standard is profound, since through its systematic use it can provide a process maturity score of from 0–15 for every supervisor and manager in government. That score will reflect their practices of standardizing a best practice for primary work activities they are responsible for, developing corresponding performance metrics that reflect the intended value of their process, and their record of involving production employees in efforts toward continuous improvement. Not only does this provide a "grade" on the state of the management of any program, it also provides a roadmap to opportunities for improvement.

But even more important is that through its systematic use it can also provide a uniform means of evaluating the management of entire departments, since senior managers (or auditors) could easily "roll-up" the results of individual program managers, to show how many of the Department's key processes are certified, and at what level.

The following shows how process certification in each unit of an agency would allow roll-up to a Department scorecard—allowing the efficiency and effectiveness of any agency to be routinely evaluated and audited. This kind of evaluation has never been possible in the past, and has the potential to revolutionize the delivery of government services.

Sample organizational scorecard, with numeric values for criteria converted to a percentage of the total possible score

Division 1	Division 2	Division 3	Division 4
90	35	45	75
65	95	80	100
75	95	85	45
25	60	65	55
65	70	90	80
70	80	65	50
		Overall organization	69.2

---

* There are many good books on structured problem solving. Perhaps the classic is *The Team Handbook*, Third Edition, (2003) by Peter R. Scholtes, Brain Joiner, and Barbara Streibel. Oriel Incorporated, Madison, WE.

4

Using the Process Management Standard

In the previous chapter we introduced the process management standard. This chapter looks at each scoring criterion and provides greater guidance to those seeking to use it on how it is scored and how it can be used to improve process efficiency and effectiveness.

STANDARD PROCESS

The first area of evaluation—Standard Process—asks the responsible manager to standardize their process and to verify that it is current and complete. It recognizes that not all processes need be standardized by a process flow chart, and some managers will prefer to use a documented procedure to do so. Regardless of the format, higher levels of process maturity depend on demonstrating its periodic update and the validation of its accuracy by those who work in the process. Several methods of doing so include demonstrating that it is up-to-date, that it is used to train new employees, and that it is linked to metrics and continuous improvement efforts.

Typically, process is standardized through development of a process flowchart that maps how the manager's designed "work stations" (not people) do the work. Each box in the flowchart should represent a task, step, or action that is clearly defined, with a known and defined input and a known and defined output. The method for doing the work reflects a best practice at the time the flowchart is completed, and the work output of each step must be articulated in a manner so that the completion of that process flow "step" could be timed, or audited. Clearly, process flow steps such as: "receive applicant file," "review applicant file," and "approve applicant file" are neither clear nor auditable.

For example, how are we to know if the applicant file contains sufficient information to be reviewed? And how are we to know what criteria are the basis of an approval versus a rejection? If these things are not apparent and defined, they can neither be timed nor audited.

This book is not intended to provide a full instructional set in process flowcharting and will simply refer those who are novice in the area to an excellent primer in the subject, *Mapping Work Processes*, by Dianne Galloway.* Process science offers many texts and tools for process analysis and improvement, and process flowcharts are the most basic of all. But while there are dozens of sub-disciplines for process improvement, from Lean to Kaizen to ISO, it is the premise of this book that mastery of simple process mapping, measurement, and continuous quality improvement are the only tasks that government must uniformly implement, system-wide. The other texts and methods have a history of making simple process management seem complex or elitist, allowing senior managers to lose focus on the simple and appropriate applications offered here.

The typical approach advised by most flow charting texts is to first create an "as is" process flowchart that defines how the process is done today, and then to devise the "will be" process flowchart that reflects discovered improvements. While not a wrong approach, the author's suggested method is to design a "could be/should be" process as the first effort. This is done because there is rarely a current and accurate process in place, and the first effort at flowcharting also provides a wealth of information about how the process *should* be done at present, and is not. The discussions that take place between those who complete the first process flowchart and those who actually work in the process also generates a wealth of information about what could be done to improve. So why not implement those simple changes at the same time

---

* ASQ Quality Press, 1994.

it is standardized? Thus, the "could be/should be" process flowcharting approach, which is generally implemented in Steps #1 and #2 listed below:

Steps to Continuous Quality Improvement

1. **Initial standardization:** Often done only by the manager, supervisor, and process experts as an idealized first version. If done by a team, it can be part of "Leveling" where a team gets together to share knowledge of the process and learn.
2. **Test and refine standard process:** Review the initial standardization with all workers in the process, and modify it to reflect their unique knowledge and the reality of production. Develop and track process measures.
3. **Identify value stream:** An analysis of all process steps to identify those that provide end-user value versus those that do not.
4. **Streamline to improve value:** Eliminate inspections, unnecessary steps, unnecessary hand-offs, and waiting.
5. **Identify sources of variation:** Typically done with the benefit of process measures. Looking for "special cause" variation that derails intended outcomes.
6. **Identify root causes of variation:** Looking for "common causes" of process variation. These will be changes and streamlining steps that will provide a steady and reliable improvement of all future process results.
7. **Continuous experimentation and creativity:** Experimentation to improve results. Could include "re-engineering." Also could be called application of the scientific method—hypothesis, study, measurement, conclusion, and implementation if feasible. Also could be Continuous Quality Improvement using SPC.
8. **Standardize and control:** Ensure that all improvements are consistently and uniformly incorporated in requirements for the future.

MEASUREMENT

Once this process of standardization and validation is set in motion, it should lead managers to a fundamental review of the process including what it is supposed to achieve—its purpose and outcome—and how its successful completion should be measured—its requirements. Those highly familiar with the principles of quality management will relate to the term customer, and the definition of customer as the user of a work output. In government it is necessary to have a broader focus, perhaps by replacing the word "customer" with the words "user," "regulated party," and "stakeholder." In government application, the successful completion of process may have to measure legitimate requirements of satisfaction of each of these parties.

An example of the need for a broader focus can be found in looking at the work of regulatory agencies. Even though the entities regulated by government (including drivers getting speeding tickets) are definitely users of a government output, they are often unwilling users of that output. They may neither value nor welcome the services provided by the regulatory authority. At the same time, a public interest group concerned with enforcement may be vitally interested in the outcome of the regulatory actions taken, even though none of the individual actions of the agency have any direct impact on that group. Likewise, the public as a whole should be beneficiaries of all regulatory enforcement.

Because of the broad focus of legitimate interests and benefits from regulatory actions, and the need to preserve rights of regulated parties, there must be a defined measurable output of each process that reflects its successful delivery of each legitimate interest, and the preservation of all rights. Taken collectively, that is the only sound basis of a customer requirement for government process. And while identification of customer in government is more difficult than in the private sector, the identification and prioritization of *all* program purposes and outcomes will serve best support that "composite customer" requirement.

As another example, the "customer" of the prison system is the inmate, but also society and the system of law. So human incarceration and rehabilitation are balanced, as is the need for uniform conformance to the system of justice. We cannot rely on the prison warden asking the prisoner if he is happy and if his needs are met, nor can we reward him if his prison population increases and each inmate stays a long time! In fact, a balanced "composite" program measure (or set of measures) is required to reflect the totality of program success.

Once each process is standardized and composite customer requirements are established for each process, these efforts must be linked to the quality of the measurements, and the overall system of process improvement— demonstrated by regular use of the scientific method.

Measurements of process are typically the most demanding because even though they are absolutely critical, there is no one perfect set of measurements. Efforts to develop a single perfect set of measures generally fail in two different ways. They fail in that workers in the process will always seek to "look good," and over time will either focus on the one attribute that is measured over others that are not measured, or they will consciously or unconsciously distort the reported numbers to show good and improved performance. In addition, the harder that management seeks to get a perfect set of numbers, the more extra work that is required to obtain the "new and improved" data.

In short, experience has taught that a fundamental set of simple, meaningful, and available numbers must be developed to align with each process, and they must be consistently tracked over time. This set must be audited to ensure its validity and a sound basis for process review. Often these measures are related to in-process activity, such as "review time," or to outputs "such as approvals per week." Other objective and valid measurements and points of measure may also be valuable and useful to management in its ultimate goal—obtaining consistent quality and/or improvement on requirements important to customers.

Validation of measures with customers is the process of obtaining structured feedback that affirms the importance of what is being measured, with a higher value placed on a method of validation that has regular and recurring methods of obtaining that feedback, and perhaps modifying some of the systems of measurement based on that learning.

Likewise, a higher value is given where two or more measures are used for management of each process, and where those measures show that outputs and outcomes have a stable and positive level of performance. For the highest scores, process performance should be within statistical "control limits," showing that the process has eliminated special causes, and hopefully, that all common cause variation is within known and acceptable levels of performance.*

While the system of measures exists to calibrate the health and performance of the process, it cannot be the sole source of information for program evaluation by the manager, or their superiors. Other factors, such as public satisfaction, employee courtesy, and a clean workplace will always be important program factors that will not, and should not,

---

* Further references on statistical process control can be found in *Juran's Quality Handbook*, 5th ed., by Joseph Juran and A. Blanton Godfrey, Sections 44 and 45.

show up on a measurement scorecard. In fact, the use of a measurement scorecard as a basis of process management should automatically disallow its use for evaluation of the individual personnel or the overall health of the program—these are different things. This is true because unless the process is kept separate of the program and its personnel there will always be a tendency to distort program activities and results. Most importantly, the factors of process performance are always most directly under the control of management and least controllable by individual workers. Even though there is a tendency of management to immediately place blame on the workers, this abdication of responsibility by managers is known to be the most damaging to overall effectiveness.

PROCESS IMPROVEMENT/EMPLOYEE EMPOWERMENT

The third basis of evaluation of process is through audit of the extent of process improvement and its associated employee empowerment. This set of evaluative criteria hinges on evidence of repetitive cycles of improvement of a process, along with a demonstrated knowledge of the process improvement effort among employees. Since it is the employees at the front line who must execute the process steps defined by a standardized best practice, their knowledge and acceptance of those steps are critical to delivered quality. Not only must they know the best practice steps that have been defined, but they must have a sense of their "right-ness." If employees feel that prescribed steps are excessive or do not make sense, they will only perform when directly supervised and will take an easier and more familiar path when they are left alone. The acknowledged best way to ensure employee ownership is to ensure their participation in the improvement process itself, through participation on process review teams and involvement in their work. At the higher levels these criteria also seek evidence showing that structured tools of analysis and learning are in place, and that continuous systematic improvement and measurable, positive results have been achieved.

The combination of the demonstrated record of improvement with employee involvement is a recognition of four factors that are critical to process management. First is the acknowledgment that any process changes must be tested for the reality of the new process design with those who actually work the process to ensure it is realistic and that it reflects their unique knowledge and the reality of production. Second, the logic of any changes must be apparent to those who run the process, or they will ignore the new instructions and return to old ways that appear more practical or personally gratifying. Third, in the long run, the best process managers are working to build a sense of ownership for the process among the workforce, so their personal commitment to quality will be a natural expression of their good work habits. Last, worker involvement and commitment create an environment where workers can and will provide ideas about further process improvements. For these reasons the two things must be connected.

More sublime reasons for worker involvement in process improvement arise from the realization that the identification of value-added and non-value-added steps in any process is not at all obvious, and often requires an active discussion and analysis by management and workers to unravel. The same is true for the identification of wasted effort. They are not readily apparent to anyone—not to managers or to workers—because most work processes in government have been around for a while, and often longer than the people who work in them. Work processes are often performed by people (including a manager) who learned how to do their part from someone else. The pattern of tasks is handed down from one to another and can be like making a copy from a photocopy, over and over again, in that the precision of the process can lose some level of detail over time.

Only when a work process is a new one is it likely that the current work unit manager will know a lot about the details of the tasks performed by each worker, and *why* they do each task in the manner they do. It is worth noting that only when there is a clear "why" can anyone evaluate whether tasks are value added or waste. That truth, however, is often buried, and business process review is often a means of "relearning" or understanding the why of each process step.

The current manager of each process *may sometimes* be truly expert in its design, but only when that individual is the one who wrote the procedure, trained staff, and created the standard forms and other support materials. In that case, the manager was the primary author of the logic for the process and would presumably keep all of that logic in their active memory for a long time afterward. When that is true, if anyone ever forgot why a particular activity was performed, that manager would remember.

The retention of the logic, or the "why" process steps are performed, can be called the "seeded logic." The seeded logic is true logic that is embedded in the job duties of the workers carrying out the process, in the flowchart (if there is one) and in the work procedures. This logic is quietly behind the scene and is like the seed of a plant in that it contains the ability to replicate perfect images of itself, even if that logic is not known by others.

If the current manager did not engineer the work process independently, another alternative is that it was established through the collective efforts of a management team, and in those instances the logic of its steps is based on decisions made by a group. In those cases, the process might have been created based on the shared knowledge and program needs of several persons. When that happens, the seeded logic may never have been apparent to current managers and workers because no one person could explain why it was created that way. If the "how" is written down, the "why" is often missing. In that instance, the workers have no choice but to assume that the steps they follow make good sense, or if they choose to abandon them they will not know what consequences may result. Making things even more complex, over the years of operation both managers and workers will come and go, so that no one will remember why things are done and the seeded logic is lost.

It is a certainty that as managers and workers come and go, the "logical order" that was first established for the process will become disrupted. So, for example, in an accounts payable process no one remembers why the person who completes the verification process and sends the invoice to the payment processing unit recorded the request in a spreadsheet. This opens another important area for review. It is not only important to maintain the process the way it is now—the way the manager first found it—it is also important to test aspects of the process to see if they still make sense. This testing of a process over time is another important part of the continuous process improvement, and it must be done as a collaborative effort of workers and the manager, to ensure that the efficiency and effectiveness of the process is retained over time.

If we look at processes as a series of steps, though, we can see a variety of inputs and outputs to the process that come from outside its sphere of control, which also adds complexity to the effort to determine whether process steps are value-added. Inputs to a process typically come from outside its span of control, for example, an application for a driver's license and an application fee. Requirements for the process—the license in this case—also come from outside its span of control, probably from a state legislature through laws. Some interim outputs of the process may go outside of the process work group—so the license fee paid may be deposited into a bank account controlled by a state controller or treasurer. Last, the approved license itself will flow to the applicant.

So, we can see that processes exist within a context that is defined by inputs, outputs, and requirements that are developed by interests outside its span of control and that may change over time. As the systems change, the ability of the process to deliver with maximum efficiency and effectiveness may be diminished, since it was designed at an earlier time. This presents the need for a manager to review and improve a process over time, which could be called responding to change, but is most frequently called process improvement.

So, let's assume there was a work process for government payment processing, and when it was first designed it was decided that the recordation of the amount and the date it was approved was important to ensure that the paper file was not lost or misplaced. In that circumstance the recordation was indeed a part of the seeded logic of the process. But over time the agency could have converted to an operational system that keeps the same information in the official operational record. So, if the spreadsheet data entry is no longer a value-added step, then the seeded logic needs change, and the step is a redundancy that should be stopped. The rule of logic here is "value-added," and it is correctly argued that non-value-added steps are waste and should be eliminated. But if no one remembers why the step was done, the step will not be recognized as a redundancy and it will continue.

It is also possible that the data recordation had no purpose in the first place and was started by someone who simply wanted a redundant record as a double check because they did not trust the operational record. Events such as these are a form of "nested logic." This is a reference to the way that a bird makes a nest, using whatever is at hand to accomplish the purpose as they see it. Many government processes are related to programs, and are unique to an office. Some process steps may be unique to a desk and worker, perhaps only with a single designated backup. Under such circumstances, the possibility for nested process steps is high.

A basic law of physics is that all things in motion tend to remain in motion, unless acted on by another force. The same is true with processes, and people tend to repeat and continue what they have seen or have been taught, unless someone tells them they should modify or stop. But who knows which is seeded logic and which is nested logic—and whether any seeded logic is out of date and no longer serves a meaningful purpose. And if no one can tell the difference, then no one knows which process steps should be retained and which should be eliminated.

More importantly, what drives the process of business process review so that candidate areas for improvement are nominated? What forces a manager to take a periodic close look at "their" process steps to determine which provide value and which are waste? That is the most significant question for process management and a primary force for process certification. Process certification has been created as a framework for process review and improvement.

And here is a key also, the efficiency and effectiveness of a process depends on intelligent oversight and development of "collective wisdom" regarding the process and its best deployment within the current work environment. The development of collective wisdom is the reason that cross-functional teams are often deployed as a part of process improvement, both because team members bring a broader and more dynamic knowledge to bear, and because they can also test whether changes will have any adverse impact. Not to mention that teams are often better at developing creative solutions, or new ways of producing the desired output, or value.

Because technology and service offerings are in continuing flux, methods that were not possible to implement in a process a year ago might be possible now. So, the need to add a new method or approach is always on the horizon. So, a primary role of process managers is to understand and "test" the process and to maintain the "collective wisdom" against which its most efficient and effective operation is measured.

The role of the manager is then threefold, to: (1) understand the original process design and maintain its design function (or "best practice") over time, (2) evaluate changes in process inputs or support systems that would make parts of the current process unnecessary or non-effective to achieve its goals and develop appropriate responses to those changes, and (3) evaluate changes to the current process, unknown in the past, that would improve the process operation in the future.

It is worthy of note that the current practice of "Lean" business process improvement is a search for waste, or alternately, for clear identification of value-add. The practice of "Six Sigma" provides a focus on performance measurement, and the development of process that will produce with greatest reliability considering those process measures. The practice of "re-engineering" often looks for new technology or methods, and the practice of ISO certification often emphasizes standardization of existing best practice. These methods add tools and methods can drive process management and continuous improvement, and the positive effects of all will be measured through the process certification standards included in this chapter.

Process control is the fundamental duty of a manager to develop and standardize a series of process steps that can be replicated by the available workforce, so that the process output is reliably achieved. Process control also implies that the manager will provide the oversight necessary to ensure that those process steps are reliably performed over time.

Process testing (or process analysis) is the continuing evaluation of the efficiency and effectiveness of the process in a changing environment, and looking for either waste or non-value-added steps that could be modified to reduce process costs or improve its results.

Process improvement is achieved by the design and testing of changes, and the restandardization of a new process logic.

More can be said about the tools and methods that could be used for each of these three, and each has a different approach, but taken together they tell us that the role of the manager is not just process control, but also process improvement. Process control and process improvement, taken together, represent process management, and *this* should be the foundation of the work of each manager. Without question, the most fundamental role of a manager is process management* and this progression of tasks is measured in the process certification guidelines provided in this chapter.

These process certification guidelines provide a tool and framework for government managers at all levels to demonstrate that their work units follow a documented best practice in primary business areas. They are structured to provide a method to evaluate and score the maturity of each process, or to be used as an audit standard. Through the uniform application of these guidelines within all agencies and offices of government, and the roll-up of scores from all its units, the public will at last benefit from an overall measure of the efficiency and effectiveness of work within each office, department, and agency. And likewise, policy makers will have the ability to see where individual offices within each department and agency are not delivering value.

---

* Author is not minimizing the importance of managing workers, but will leave that subject to another text.

5

Structured System Management

In the previous chapters we presented work processes, and noted that those processes provide the specific services and defined work outcomes of government. Processes in turn are run by the legions of hard-working and well-intentioned supervisors and managers, and the employees who work for them in hundreds or thousands of work offices around the world. These are the people the public typically will see and will often blame for a poor result. Management systems, on the other hand, reflect the end result of the work of their bosses—the chief executives, department directors, program office managers—who make up the "Executive Management" of government agencies. These are the folks in the executive suite or corner offices of our government buildings, who are best known by the elected representatives and not by the public. And while the work of executive and program office managers is typically *not* seen by the public, and is rarely found to be a source of blame for poor performance, its role is definitional for *all* the work of government. Mysteriously, the work that such executive managers do is often seen as above analysis, and some kind of vague extension of the executive persona. This book will directly challenge that belief, and introduces a system of structured system management in government as a missing link for its excellent performance.

This new practice of structured system management focuses on the fact that all management work creates value, and that the value can be *defined*. When it is, we can see that there is an expectation that chief executives, department directors, and program office managers all support the work of the organization, which is done in processes. We call the work output of those managers systems, and we can look at those systems as if they were just high-level processes (or "macro" processes) that sit "on top" of localized, value-creating processes lower in the organization. Just like processes, systems need to be defined and standardized, and run in a way that can be studied, evaluated, and improved over time. Put most simply, management systems provide a logical structure and pattern for what will be done, and supports those processes with inputs, resources, and permissions.[*]

If a process is likened to an electrical appliance—such as a computer tablet—there are three systems on which its performance must directly depend. First is an electric utility that brings power into the home. Second is the in-home electrical system made up of circuits, wall switches, electrical plugs, and circuit breakers that bring the power to the cord. Third are the cable or satellite content providers that generate the desired input signal. These systems are entirely outside of the tablet, but each must support its proper operation, and each has a defined output that can be measured. If any of these systems does not function, the tablet cannot do its job. The same is true with the management systems that must serve and support front-line business processes. Those front-line processes often depend on authorizations, personnel, decisions, or other kinds of support that are provided by higher-level management systems.

Systems, then, are the organizational context in which processes exist. They are real, they exist to create a defined outcome (or purpose), they do require preliminary actions or steps which can be defined, they can be mapped, their outputs can be measured, and they are subject to learning and improvement.[†]

The best organizational systems can be managed in the same way as are processes with a group of standardized practices and actions that are believed to be "best practice." In this way important organizational systems become a *deliberate construction* of management. For that to happen this chapter will focus on helping to identify where they exist, and how to improve them. The system management standard (introduced in this chapter) provides a structure for that investigation and looks at the logic that defines structure and operations. Even though system operation can be done formally (through rules, policy, and guidelines) or informally (through periodic directives, statements, and understandings), this standard recognizes documented systems as superior. That is presumed true because documentation facilitates awareness, requires focused attention

---

[*] Systems science attempts to understand humans and their environment as part of their interacting with the forces of nature, and learning to predict positive outcomes based on that understanding. The word *systems* in this book will be limited to management systems, which is the science of how government leaders and managers seek to control fiscal resources, human resources, information, supplies, authorities, and procedures under their direct and indirect control, in order to ensure better organizational results. The complexity of systems is discussed again in the introduction of Chapter 6.

[†] See *Lean System Management for Leaders*, R. Mallory (2018), Taylor & Francis/CRC Press.

to create, and supports predictable effective use by everyone in the organization. It also allows for evaluation and measurement of results, with learning and improvement over time.

The alternative to systems—their polar opposite—is leadership that provides all its process support spontaneously and unpredictably, or by extrapolating past practice to the future. This kind of "leadership" makes all its significant organizational decisions in real-time, without input from those affected, and outside of any kind of predictable or logical framework. Where systems are lacking nothing is predictable and the criteria for decision-making is whatever the executive "thinks" at the moment the decision is made. This kind of chaos is obviously not supportive of the reliable production of results.

The budget development system of a government entity, for example, might be defined in a formal policy, or informally structured through an annual announcement by the executive officer. It is much more likely that the logic and utility of the formal policy will be much greater, as will its predictable and effective use.

The structured definition and management of systems also holds executive managers accountable for meeting the "requirements" of subordinate processes, since we can now see that the systems are either suppliers to processes, or customers of their outputs. (See Figure 5.1).

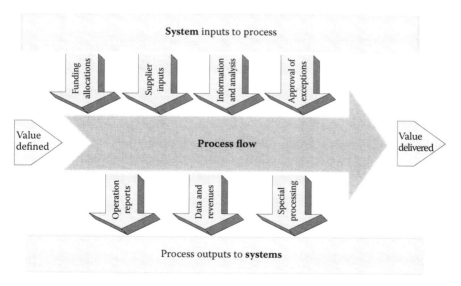

FIGURE 5.1
System and process, inputs and outputs.

Systems reflect and provide the required inputs and outputs of processes, connect those processes end-to-end, and to the business systems and reporting of the agency. The evaluation of systems is based on how completely and how well it brings together its processes into an aligned and effective organization.

Structured systems can be as simple as a policy or rule, and as complex as operational handbooks or an "if/then" decision tree. In good organizations, important systems are documented, cataloged, and current, and in bad ones, they are unstated and assumed to be understood and are discovered by those who need them only when they are reprimanded for not following the rules. However, it is the structured and "recorded" that are likely to be most useful and to drive excellence in the whole organization. These systems are managed with a purpose: Sustaining, supporting, and defining best practices and optimal results. For this reason, recorded systems will be the focus of this standard.

Figure 5.1 (preceding page) shows a process nested in organizational systems, with systems controlling and supporting its work, and with the process in turn providing required outputs to either customers, or to other systems.* In effect, the process is a working unit within an organization defined systems. In this context, it is obvious why documented and logical systems are critical to excellent organizational results.

Structured system management is the "imprint" of a logical and effective leadership system and is the capstone work of the executive management. It presents a business case or value proposition, with its primary strategies, structure, and the major operational processes used to execute the model. It begins by providing mission and objectives, which reflect the business purpose of the office and leadership position—including why it exists and what it must achieve. This is the definition of the outcomes it is commissioned to create, through a series of actions and activities (or "operations") that are believed to be the necessary steps to those defined outcomes. Since the structured system created must support a business purpose, the purpose and outcome are needed before the principal activities and actions needed to achieve that value.

Mission and agency objectives are *the* starting point for all systems development because they provide the necessary foundation for all operational

---

* It is important to note, however, that since systems are run by "higher ups" in government organizations, the requirements to be met can be arbitrary or changeable (and therefore a root cause of waste) if they are not made consistent with the principles of Lean and quality science.

activity. They are also foundational to development of a complete business plan* that should define the operational plan for the organization overall, and for each unit. In reality, though, very few government organizations and units actually do define an operational plan, outside of mapping a few specific processes, which underlines the reason for structured system management and its matching practice of system mapping as presented here.

The development of a business plan that defines systems is not a novel concept, and two comprehensive means of doing so that are already well-known are the International Standards Organization (ISO) 9001 standards,[†] and the Criteria for Performance Excellence issued by the U.S. Baldrige Performance Excellence Program.[‡]

The ISO 9000 family of standards is an auditable third-party standard, which certifies the existence and use of quality management systems in applicant organizations. While broadly recognized as effective, implementation of this standard has been difficult and expensive in organizations, and often has been seen as overly complex and not fully applicable in many branches of government. In addition, required fees for copies of the ISO standards, and for third-party certifications, makes it difficult for government to use.

The Baldrige Criteria for Performance Excellence is a U.S. national performance award and standard. Its seven categories provide an *integrated approach* to organizational performance management and excellence and require applicants to document an approach and deployment of operational methods in six category areas[§] including:

- Leadership (including "governance")
- Strategic planning
- Customer focus
- Information and analysis
- Process management
- Human resource focus

---

* The same concept was described a "business model" as in the book by Gerard George and Adam J. Bock, The Business Model in Practice and its Implications for Entrepreneurship Research, *Entrepreneurship Theory and Practice*, Vol. 35, No. 1, 2011, pp. 83–111.

† The International Organization for Standardization (ISO) is an international standard-setting body composed of representatives from various national standards organizations, and publishes several quality management standards in which organizations, including government entities, can seek third-party certification of its quality management system. ISO is headquartered in Geneva, Switzerland. Its web address is www.iso.org.

‡ See www.nist.gov/baldrige.

§ The names of the categories have been slightly modified over the years of the award, and the author has used some category titles from previous years where believed to be more descriptive.

The seventh category asks applicants to document for business results.

The use and certification of a government agency through either of these quality frameworks is one way to demonstrate the highest levels of systems maturity in executive management, but it is also noted that other systems or a different list of systems may be equally useful, or much more useful depending on the nature of each organization. In actual practice, the strong suggestion that only certain defined systems are important to organizations can drive a one-size fits all philosophy that drives executive leaders to engage in work and meetings that are not useful, while missing others that are crucially important. It may also exempt an entire category of leadership from having to define their systems because they are not on the predetermined list of the currently acknowledged frameworks.

This latter category includes both program office managers and project management office managers, both of whom will obtain enormous benefit from system management, as will their organizations. This is true for two reasons:

First, the use of structured system management forces managers to first define their best known operational practice (based on the documented outputs they need to provide) and then to document and plan an achievable best practice to accomplish those objectives. This becomes a measurable plan from which results can be objectively ascertained and from which learning and improvement can be implemented.

Second, the documentation of each system will invite the identification of inputs to the system (where it is the customer of another process or system), the actions and activities that create its value, and the outputs of the system (where it is the supplier of something of value to another process or system). In this way, the system can be reviewed for waste, delay, and non-value-added steps using the practices of Lean quality improvement, and the performance of the entire organization can be fine-tuned. The identification of inputs and outputs of every system will clarify requirements and align *all* the work flows of the organization, assisting in continuous work flow and the creation of value-added work.*

Starting at the top of the organization and looking down, the systems identified as "key" for first mapping should refer to its business plan. In this manner, the organization may say that the use of Lean practices, quality assurance, innovation, or research and development are most

---

* A detailed guide to creating structured system management is provided in the book, *Lean System Management for Leaders*, by Richard Mallory.

important to its future. If so, it should have a structured pattern of practice (also known as a "system") in mind to accomplish those goals. Likewise, excellent organizations should have a system of oversight and a system of resource allocation in place.

While the establishment and tracking of many systems may sound like a lot of work, it will not be because each structured system will be delegated down to the manager who is now accountable for that work output. The genius of key system mapping is to only track those systems whose outputs are critical to the organization and to ask those who are responsible for that work to create and report on the system in place. In this way, your organization will be placing accountability and authority in the same place.

If each executive office engages in a review of its business plan and strategic objectives as a first means of identifying its key systems, it will ensure that its managers are prepared to confront the specific challenges they are meant to address.* Based on this kind of needs articulation, the systems created might define and support management reporting and business controls or provide necessary resources such as trained personnel, contractor services, or IT systems.

Executive leaders must decide whether some or all of the above best support and control the business plan and its core business practices. Because the components of systems management are discretionary, it is important that executive management select a group of components that are organizationally important and in greatest alignment with desired results. It is also worthy of note that not *all* executive leaders will participate in *all* systems definitions, and just one (or several) senior executive could fully define an important organizational system. Human resource management and information technology management could be examples of that.

Indeed, senior leaders may get the *best* results if they ask every manager in every branch and office to develop a list of specific outcomes that *they* are responsible for, with a matching business purpose for their office. This will help to "name" the key system that needs to be defined. It can also then be built-out by identifying a series of principal activity groups that are necessary to contribute the "value-add" of that system (or office), as shown by the keystone shapes in Figure 5.2. Finally, the actions and

---

* Organization-wide strategies may cross areas of executive responsibility, which will require system mapping that is similar to cross-functional process mapping—it may require collaboration across organizational boundaries.

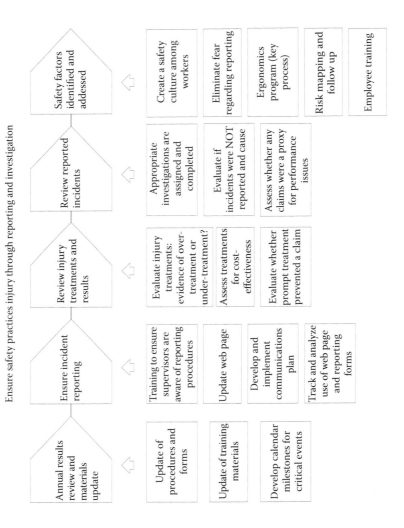

FIGURE 5.2
Example of a system map.

activities that contribute to or cause success in each principal activity group can also be created, providing a summary "operational plan." If metrics are developed to reflect success or failure of important interim steps, or of system outputs, we then have a system map with much of the functionality of a process map, and which can be used to analyze current performance and improve future performance. An example of such a system map, is provided on the opposite page.

The system management standard was developed to provide a uniform and objective means of feedback regarding whether managers are fulfilling their business purpose and reliably delivering the value-add that the organization expects. It can therefore tell senior management whether subordinate managers have developed and documented an operational plan to accomplish their goals.

Use of the system management standard on an organizational basis seeks to confirm that an agency has methods to ensure the quality of its necessary organizational systems, across the board, and on a sustained basis. It does not mandate any one system's structure and assumes that the executive management of each agency will logically analyze its own goals, value creating processes, organizational inter-relationships, and best practices, and will select a set of key systems for its management.

Just as with process management, it is recognized that system management provides a tool that can enhance predictable value. And just as with process management, it is recognized that the use of this tool and the refinement of key systems takes time, and so must produce measurable results. Trying to define and standardize everything is as bad as defining and standardizing nothing. A basic rule of quality is that analysis, planning, and standardization of best practices will generate results, while the failure to implement known best practice and to learn from the past will drive error, waste, and failure. It is certain that the standardization and control of key systems is necessary for sustained, long-term efficiency and effectiveness—and value. This again refers to the primary goal of auditable standards in government—which is the enhancement of value, efficiency, and effectiveness—its VE-2.

6

Using the Structured System Management Standard

The system management standard introduces something new to organizational management because with its use the work of executive management is no longer invisible. Currently there is no real-time dashboard indicator of the quality of executive management in government agencies. The current situation is like having an automobile for which the owner does not keep its service record, nor check the oil level, air pressure, or the engine temperature. The only way we will know if its maintenance is being done well is if it is *not* being done well and there is an obvious breakdown! Typically, we learn of lapses in executive management only when there is a massive and very public lawsuit or failure, and a multi-year follow-up study finds that malfeasance occurs.

To be fair, the U.S. federal government does have an Office of the Inspector General that does periodic agency audits, and most state and local entities have similar kinds of audit offices that perform similar reviews. But these reviews are usually conducted on a random basis and often focused on a single program or process, and do not provide comprehensive and prospective indicators of problems. They are often scatter-shot reviews that address individual agency offices often from the perspective of a single problem. They do not and cannot validate the proper management of an entire organization.

In addition, because theses audits are conducted by persons only broadly familiar with the programs they audit, their recommendations can be prescriptive, documentary, or educated guesses about problem resolution. While this current audit structure does provide a stop-gap means of eliminating fraud and abuse, it is not preventative as is system management.

The structured systems management standard provides a new approach to executive and program office functions because it looks for the existence of an operational plan, the documentation of the attributes of success or failure in each component of that plan, and the development of metrics and indicators to correspond to each component.

It provides several actionable categories for system documentation and its performance measurements, for the design of action plans to address system variables and risk, and to show the periodic review and improvement of operational plans. It allows for a scoring of progress (or "maturity") in each criteria area, and through that analysis, the next steps to developing better control over system functions. The standard is based on four criteria areas and scoring criteria as noted in Table 6.1, which is a summary version of the standard developed by the American Society for Quality Government Division.*

Table 6.1 shows the category areas, and the progression of each scoring criteria area, from a numeric score of "0" to a score of "5."

System purpose and structure refers to whether the value of the system has been defined, and whether the principal actions and activities that define that system operational plan have been considered and documented. In other words, has the management group that "owns" this system focused on what the end result of its activity must be, and who is the next user of its output? These questions define the purpose or "aim" of the system, its output requirements, and its operational plan. One way of detailing a system operational plan is through a system map, such as the one shown in Figure 5.1.

Important to the operational structure of the system is an order, pattern, and purpose, and one thing that makes this challenging is that senior managers do not always control all of the personnel from whom they must get help and cooperation. This means that obtaining recognition of the group dependencies and clarifying roles (through feedback and agreements) becomes very important. In this way, system structuring is a bit like project team management, in that it requires cooperation and communication to succeed.

It will be a great help to have hoped for results (or "outputs") defined, and general recognition of both the key actions in the operational plan and its milestones. In this way, the system manager is using an approach and

---

* The system management standard, complete version, is available at: http://asq.org/gov in the reference material section.

TABLE 6.1

Summary of Criteria—System Management Standard

Systems Purpose and Structure

0 – The system is named and has known purpose, but no structure. Specific system actions, events, and activities respond to outside influences and may be based on political agendas or individual judgements, without regard to analysis or past learning experience.

5 – There is documented evidence of an ordered system that delivers uniform and predictable quality outputs over multiple operational cycles. The ordered system is supported by a system map and supporting documents covering all tasks, accountabilities, and contributing factors. Major intervening variables and system risks have been identified. The system map links to process maps as necessary, to accomplish organizational goals, and requirements statements for process inputs or outputs are built into systems requirements. System deployment is specific to the means used to manage the system and to ensure its continuing operations according to design. Operational deployment is supported by responsibilities and accountability for each contributing resource group, and using indicators and performance measures for all principal activity groups. There is evidence of the use of this system management structure for three or more years.

Goal Directedness through Measures and Feedback

0 – The system has no clearly defined outcomes, and no expectations for its performance. Its hoped-for outcomes are ambiguous.

5 – Performance feedback and objective measures are linked to this system and all its defined activity groups. Positive levels and trends exist for the entire system and for all its principal activities. Several indicators and measures are available for each defined activity group. There is evidence that the performance of this defined system has improved and contributed to improving organizational outcomes over three or more years.

Management of Intervening Variables and Risk

0 – Intervening variables and risk have not been identified or are unknown.

5 – The risk management plan is analyzed and reviewed at least annually. System design and structure has been modified to lessen the impact or occurrence of intervening variables and risks. There is documented evidence of the use of analysis to lessen risk and system impacts. Root cause analysis is used to design risk management plans. There is documented evidence of systems learning and improvement.

Alignment, Evaluation, and Improvement

0 – There are no systematic efforts to learn and improve. The resources and personnel that constitute the system do not recognize its existence.

5 – There is evidence of continuous systematic annual improvement, participated in by all defined systems personnel. Responsibilities, accountability, consultation, and informing roles have been identified for each primary activity group and for dependent tasks and activities. There are measurable, positive results on outcomes and in each activity group, with demonstrated positive relationship to all dependent processes.

deployment to make the system clear and to ensure it obtains its intended results. There are lots of ways that systems in organizations can suffer, and two of the most crippling are the failure to clearly define why they exist and what they are intended to accomplish.

Goal directedness builds off the definition of hoped for system results and outputs, as defined by its output requirements. It is recognized that the ultimate output of systems is sometimes difficult to quantitatively measure (e.g., how can you score a completed budget document?). Because of this, the system management standard asks whether metrics and indicators (collectively called "measures") are linked to either the principal activity areas or its known driving factors. This is done through providing descriptions of the positive and negative attributes of each principal activity group identified in the system map. So, for example, if a budget system has identified obtaining and considering division needs as a part of its system, we can measure the completion of our meeting schedule according to milestone dates, and the use of an analytic method to evaluate priorities, needs, and options. We might also identify that "missed needs" would be a negative consequence of the "obtaining and considering division needs" activity group, and we could measure after-the-fact emergency funding requests as a negative system indicator.

In other words, how we can create focused attention on objective and measurable attributes of system success, both at the final system outcome and within its principal activity groups, and these measures can and will provide us with a comprehensive scorecard of system success. This will allow us to use ongoing performance feedback to understand what works, what does not, and to develop continuous improvement within our system. It will provide us the basis of learning and innovation.

Management of intervening variables and risk asks whether those factors that are most likely to disrupt the optimal system design plan have been identified and addressed. In Chapter 2 we discussed the unifying theory of work management, which states that processes are controllable in large part because the people, methods, and resources used to produce work outputs are both predictable and defined and under the direct control of a closely defined team of people. In addition, they are produced in a work environment that can be organized and protected. Of all these factors, many will not be true for systems, and in fact, the work output provided in each system cycle may also have a lot of variation. So, for example, a budget plan produced in a year of political crisis may differ greatly from one produced in a year where there is no crisis and no new priorities. Indeed, there could be a lot of variation in the required budget plan resulting only from a change of leadership.

This discussion highlights the fact that systems must be managed in an environment where there may be significant intervening variables, and risks from a variety of sources. This criterion then asks managers to identify the known and most likely intervening variables, and to conduct risk analysis to determine an appropriate response. While in some circumstances it may require changes to the system map to prevent the problems caused by one kind of variable, the development of procedures or scenario analysis may be best for response to a different kind of variable. This criterion group challenges system managers to use data and root cause analysis to evaluate whether prevention or mitigation can be built into the system design, and to use other forms of risk management where a prevention strategy is not available.

Alignment, evaluation, and improvement asks to see whether the system goes through annual evaluation, improvement, and change, to reflect learning gained through its continuing operations, and its periodic structured review. The learning and improvement activity is only made possible through documentation of system requirements and its best practice operational plan, and through tracking of the established indicators and metrics. Its success is also facilitated by the development of requirements throughout its value creation work flow, both for process outputs and for supply inputs, to ensure the smooth and predictable creation of intended value. The system operational plan itself must also align, both with other systems in the organization and with processes. Efforts to ensure alignment in all key linkages will drive organizational success at the highest level. The use of root cause analysis for all identified issues will support structured learning and improvement.

The system management standard allows for a measure of system capacity—the likelihood that it will reliably deliver its intended value. This can be done by system audit, using the system management standard.* The use and application of the system management standard allows each system to be ranked from a score of "0" to "20," with scores expressed either in those terms or as a percentage of the 20 points possible. The latter method will allow consistent scoring of system and process maturity results throughout an organization, and it will support a rollup of the scoring of all key processes and systems within each division or unit and in the organization

---

* See Appendix A.

overall. In this manner, an agile and comprehensive framework for quality practice implementation is also possible.

Overall, use of the system management standard will push executive management to annually evaluate defined systems, to test them for positive results, and to look for continuous improvement of all systems.

7

Aligned Leadership Objectives

Aligned leadership objectives are designed to promote accountability for results at the top level of government, in a political leadership system in which there appears to be little accountability at the present time. The introduction of this book cites the conventional wisdom that government is *not* efficient and *not* effective, that it costs too much, and that no one knows where to start to fix it. Aligned leadership objectives are where to start to fix it because such objectives must define what the government agency is supposed to be doing, as a point of reference and comparison. This is particularly important with government because unlike private business, which must sell its products and services to willing customers, government could decide to do anything or everything.

Government has no naturally correcting mechanism to match its activities to resources, and instead it can choose to deliver poor service in many areas instead of good service in a few. This is a principal reason for use of the aligned leadership objectives standard because it will initiate a discussion about what every government entity is being asked to do, and will encourage those agencies to update those objectives regularly.

Just as Article 1, Section 8 of the U.S. Constitution gives Congress the power to adopt any law for the "general welfare" of the country, most government jurisdictions are only limited in the number of things they do by the amount of money they can spend (and borrow). There is almost no limit to the range of possibilities that can be undertaken, and most governments (like people) must continually balance between what they would like to do against what they can do. The problem here is that no individual or entity has a singular vested interest in trying to reduce the number of things government is asked to do,* and as it takes on more things there is a commensurate interest in increasing taxes to pay for it all.

Actually, the only pervasive and organic motivation for government is to grow,† since the elected representatives to each government body generally bring many ideas for new measures and view their own success in terms of getting them approved. This creates a natural tendency of all governments to accumulate an overburden of things to do, which is magnified by the mandates of many existing laws, often with focused implementation demanded by court orders.

Even though most corporate Chief Executive Officers and their Board of Directors develop aligned leadership objectives every year, it is amazing in contrast that the U.S. Congress does not. In too many instances in present times partisan political leaders fight about everything and agree on nothing. Most importantly, they fail to agree on or adopt any consolidated goals for the government for which they are responsible. Perhaps the most visible failure is that of the U.S. Congress, which does not even try to adopt national priorities or a consistent scorecard to measure results against those goals. Because there are no national goals, the annual goals of each agency are determined only through past authorizations—which in many cases are decades old—and by annual appropriations and "continuing resolutions" that often simply divide the fiscal pie in a pro-rata manner. It is a formula for mediocre performance, which is focused on someone showing why the model of the past is wrong, instead of presenting a current model, based on perceived future needs.

Where elected leaders do not agree among themselves what the agency is supposed to do, then the agency head will be trying to do too many things and without appropriate resources for all, in hopes of showing that efforts were made in all legally required areas. Because of the unclear goals and over-reaching, it would not be a surprise that the end results will also be questionable, or that the agency might be found to be wasting resources because less-than-optimal methods of achieving program goals might be in place.

---

* While a variety of audit agencies, cost control commissions, sunset laws, and fiscal departments are asked to look for "waste, fraud, and abuse," these are targeted and singular efforts that often are relegated to the second tier of legislative interests. Their cumulative impact in reducing the size of government has been far less than the collective impact of new laws and court orders to increase program size and spending.

† This is further discussed in Chapter 9, under the heading "End Incentives for Building Bureaucracy."

It is implied that the goals and objectives of every government organization are clear and understood, but in government this is far from the truth. Even though most of the objectives and "purpose" statements of government agencies are prescribed by law, in many cases those enactments were implemented many years ago and have been amended many times since. Where these laws have been amended the changes have been made like patches on old garments so that the original intent and design is now uncertain. So, for example, the U.S. Rural Electrification Administration was first established as a response to the Great Depression in 1935, to bring telephones and electric service to a predominately rural U.S. population. But in the year 2018, long after all the rural versus urban population balance has reversed, all rural areas are on an electrical grid, and corded telephones are mostly obsolete, the agency still exists! Indeed, many legislative changes have been made and it now operates as the USDA Rural Utilities Service.* It is not uncommon for all government agencies to have very broad mandates, with many of its original goals at least partially obsolete.

As another example, the mission of the Department of Labor is to "foster, promote, and develop the welfare of the wage earners, job seekers, and retirees of the United States; improve working conditions; advance opportunities for profitable employment; and assure work-related benefits and rights." Clearly, though, there are a lot of program areas that could fall in that span of control, even though its success must depend on achievement of a critical few.

Two other sources of unclarity are the result of oversight hearings and court decisions. So, hearings by elected officials and stated public criticisms of agencies by elected lawmakers have the effect of establishing or prioritizing new goals of agencies. Because of such hearings, a police department in a city that has had an outbreak of dog bites might be asked to assist animal control units with the identification and capture of loose animals. And while this is not a bad thing in itself, it could be if the police chief had to pull units that were assisting with investigative activities.

Court orders can be the result of litigation based on many causes of action, and one end result of such an action would be a court order to do a particular thing, or be found in contempt.

---

* There are powerful forces for the continuation of all government programs, and a general unwillingness of civil servants to point out areas for economy, that are discussed further in Chapter 8, under the heading "End Incentives for Building Bureaucracy."

Different parties can and do ask various government agencies to undertake multiple goals and activities, and agency heads are often uncertain which goal or priority is more important than any other. In this situation, they must make a series of judgment calls about exactly how to allocate resources to meet all possible expectations. While this kind of uncertainty about purpose can be expected to be a part of the job of an agency head, what should not be a part of the job is a failure of the overseeing elected body to establish a clear set of goals and objectives, to ask for performance reporting on achievement of those goals, and to take responsibility for achievement of those stated results.

Especially when foundational legislation is a patchwork and where courts have muddied the water, there is no one else to speak for the unified public good than elected officials. This is the focus of the audit standard of aligned system objectives—that its excellence of its services will be in direct relation to the existence of a clear set of goals and objectives that are part of a performance scorecard, and for which the elected representatives are held personally accountable.

Objectives, like goals, provide direction and the more precisely they describe the desired future, the better the direction. A wise man once said that if you don't know where you are going, then any road will get you there. The opposite statement is also true: The only way to arrive at a particular destination that is important to you is to select the one road that leads to that destination. The adoption of a series of specific objectives that are focused on primary measurable outcomes will have the positive effect of focusing the resource base of each jurisdiction on the things that are most important, and calling attention to those that are not on the list.

It is certain that if leaders cannot first agree on what the government is to achieve in fairly specific terms, then no wonder they do not get it! The fundamental problem of ineffective government then is the first step—leaders cannot first define what effective government would do in comparison.

Aligned leadership objectives are the third of three auditable standards, and report on the existence of consensus objectives (or goals), and whether elected officials have agreed on goals for their jurisdiction, clearly communicated those goals to senior leaders of their government, confirmed how government leaders will accomplish those goals in each major department, and implemented a scorecard for the results that are expected. While the standard does not require that this all happens annually, annual completion of this cycle achieves the highest point scores.

Adoption of this standard will correct any mission drift or unclarity. It has several other significant and positive effects. Most important is that it will require the elected representatives and agency heads to take a collective look forward, replacing a current bias toward the past view. Obtaining a joint agreement on objectives for the entire jurisdiction and for each agency, with prioritized measurable goals, must also be forward looking. Creation of a scorecard of outcomes with associated measures will require a long-term focus—in contrast to what occurs in many jurisdictions today.

Lastly, this process will provide a "progressive elaboration" of agency metrics that will correct any unintentional bias in operational focus. A May 2006 article in *Harvard Business Review** gave an excellent example of an unintended drift in operational focus as follows: "When Joseph Dear became the assistant secretary of labor (and head of OSHA) in 1993 OSHA measured success chiefly in terms of the number of inspections conducted and fines imposed. While in certain situations inspections and fines were the appropriate response, they were not the only, and sometimes not the most effective way of advancing OSHA's mission." The article went on to say that the metrics—which were the most measurable outputs available in 1993—eventually created an unintended situation where employees felt they were not recognized for efforts to obtain safe workplaces through education or voluntary compliance.

Even though it is recognized that the long-term tracking of measurable goals is the only valid way to demonstrate agency value, it is also recognized that an unintended drift in operational goals is a not-uncommon side-effect. This can only be corrected through a necessary management dynamic that requires the regular review of measurable goals and the realignment with those goals with hoped-for objectives. This typically requires the development of some new measures and the elimination of some old measures on an annual basis. This can and should be accomplished through completion of aligned leadership objectives.

Creation of aligned leadership objectives within a jurisdiction will also provide a report card for elected officials that will ultimately connect political promises to demonstrated results. Its requirements can be met through collaboration between the Chief Executive and the legislative body of every government entity to adopt its primary goals and objectives[†]

---

* "Change Management in Government," by Frank Ostroff. *Harvard Business Review*, May 2006. p. 142.

[†] The standard does not intend that agencies articulate every goal and objective, especially when many requirements are expressed in voluminous code from many past years. It is intended that each agency articulate its primary goals as a means of ensuring proactive leadership. Where conflicts over resources necessary develop, it may then behoove governments to review past goals and requirements, and where they do not match with future goals consider them for elimination.

(hopefully in priority order) and to describe the desired future state associated with that.

This does not seem unreasonable since each elected representative has already run for office on a series of promises, which should be in writing somewhere. The only difficulty is in converting political promises, or "positions" into "objectives" as defined in this standard. That term may be foreign to many partisan office holders since it is a description of a desired future state or characteristic. It is a description of *what* is to be accomplished, rather than *how*. In addition, political partisans typically express goals in terms of being opposed to things, like tax increases or air pollution, rather than in favor of objectives such as a balanced budget or a "safe" air quality standard. The difference between the typical political "position" and an objective is that the objective is intended to describe a desired future state or impact. It cannot be vague or accusatory like "ending wasteful spending" or "fighting tax breaks" because there is no specific way to objectively measure words like "wasteful" or "fighting" without additional definition. Specific spending requests would also not qualify as "objectives" since they are a reflection of "how" to accomplish something. They would need to be reworded to express objectives.

So, for example, the current debate about the implementation of a U.S. national health care system would need annual agreement from Congress on an objective (or objectives) regarding positive outcomes of our health care system on which all could agree. So perhaps it would need to be rephrased as "universal coverage," "easier access to health insurance," "stabilizing costs of health insurance," or "stabilizing costs of health care." Despite the partisan acrimony, it must be possible to agree on some shared health care objective—and if that can be done then progress can be measured. And until that can be done the public cannot tell what the benefit of the investment really is or if a given action like "Obamacare" is working.

While this vision of aligned system objectives is probably far different from what is considered realistic today, that is the point—a significant change must occur to achieve an excellent return from the public investment in government. It is significant that elected leaders are fiduciary officials for the public—that they have the primary legal responsibility for ensuring that value is received for financial resources provided. Therefore, holding them responsible for results is both fair and reasonable. The fact that elected leaders have convinced the public that it is not fair to hold them accountable or that it is impossible to hold them accountable has been one of the greatest tragedies of modern political democracy. This is a shield that must be removed, and the aligned systems objective standard must be the first step in bringing this about.

There is a humorous definition of committee as "a group of the unwilling, chosen from the unfit, to do the unnecessary," and with a few modifications that may well fit the impression that most people have of their federal and state legislatures. This should not be true, of course, and might not be if objectives were made clear, and results were reported. It would certainly give voters a chance to hold political leaders accountable, which is the primary intent of the aligned leadership objectives standard. The theory is that if voters know whether aligned leadership objectives exist, they will respond appropriately. The fundamental assumption of this argument is that democratic institutions *can* create consensus goals, and while the values and behaviors of some voters may have to change to ensure that happens, it seems as if it should be easily achievable.

It is worth note that in cities and counties throughout America, where partisan politics is perhaps least invasive and voters are perhaps most knowledgeable, it is often the case that consolidated goals are routinely agreed on in an annual strategic plan, budget plan, or both. So, for example, the Board of Directors of a regional park district in California has for the past several years adopted goals for each of its departments within its budget document, that are also then deployed as the annual operational goals. In the process of adoption, all goals are aligned with the district's mission statement and "Master Plan." Any new objectives are presented by either the general manager or board members, and the board reviews, updates, and adopts both the objectives and associated annual goals as a part of its annual board workshops. Indeed, there are many cities, counties, and special districts that follow a similar path on an annual basis.

The biggest apparent disconnect is at the state and federal levels. It is there that such consolidated goals are least often agreed on, and where sometimes almost nothing other than argument seems to take place.

The aligned leadership objective standard is shown in Table 7.1.

TABLE 7.1

Aligned Leadership Objectives Standard

Annual Statement of Objectives and Goals	Linkage to Operational and Tactical Planning	Scorecard Development and Use
0 – Elected officials do not adopt objectives and goals, other than what is provided in law.	0 – There is no linkage between objectives and goals developed by elected officials and agency operational and tactical planning.	0 – Elected officials do not provide any structured scorecard for the public.
1 – Elected officials adopt some objectives and goals, but not systematically and for all agencies, and not annually.	1 – Some linkage exists between elected officials and agency operational and tactical planning.	1 – Some annual results of agencies are published in a scorecard.
2 – Objectives and goals exist for all agencies, but are not prioritized and do not have measurable goals.	2 – One-third to half of all agencies link annual operational planning to legislative priorities for action, which are formally or informally expressed.	2 – One-third to half of all agencies present results in an annual published scorecard.
3 – An annual statement of objectives and goals is developed for all agencies and for the jurisdiction, but it is not prioritized and does not have measurable goals associated with them.	3 – Most agencies link operational and tactical planning to priorities formally provided by elected officials. A system exists for formally soliciting suggestions on simplification of mandates.	3 – Most agencies have results presented in an annual scorecard, that is based on the annual statement of objectives and goals for the jurisdiction.

(Continued)

TABLE 7.1 (CONTINUED)

Aligned Leadership Objectives Standard

Annual Statement of Objectives and Goals	Linkage to Operational and Tactical Planning	Scorecard Development and Use
4 – A statement of objectives and goals is developed for all agencies and for the jurisdiction on an annual basis, and for two years or more. All objectives and goals are prioritized and have measurable goals.	4 – An annual statement of objectives and goals is communicated to each agency annually by elected officials, in a timely manner. After creation, some are reviewed again by elected officials who can recommend simplifications of mandates and program requirements.	4 – The annual scorecard includes performance measures for all agencies and for the jurisdiction, and it has been published for two years or more.
5 – The statement of objectives and goals meets all requirements of Level 4, has been in place for 3–5 years, and the objectives and goals are unanimously adopted, or adopted by a consensus voting system.	5 – An annual statement of objectives and goals is communicated to each agency annually by elected officials, in a timely manner, so that it can be used by each agency to develop a corresponding annual operational and tactical plan. Each agency operational and tactical plan is reviewed and adopted with or without changes by elected officials, or a subcommittee of the elected body, and used as a primary reference in the review of budget requests, and/or revision of goals. There is a continuing system for simplification of mandates and program requirements at the request of departments.	5 – This list of objectives and goals is used to develop a performance scorecard for each agency and for the Chief Executive Officer at the end of that year. The performance scorecards are adopted by unanimous vote or consensus. Each legislative body publishes the scorecard associated with the agencies that it reviewed and approved, with members taking accountability for results. Level 5 scoring will be associated with tracking of consistent metrics for the entire jurisdiction and for each agency over 3–5 years.

8

Auditable Standards
as a Catalyst for the Future

The transformation of government envisioned by this book will come about when the annual financial audit required in every local, state, and federal government is accompanied by a Certified Public Quality Audit using the standards introduced here. The ASQ Government Division (http://asq.org/gov) is committed to pursuit of that goal in future years, and has established a Center for Auditable Quality Standards in Government to provide consistency in auditor training and maintain uniformity in the application of auditable standards in the future.

In addition, it is recognized that many jurisdictions may prefer to conduct self-audits, and to train internal auditors to evaluate key processes and systems. Both the process management standard and the system management standard should be easy to use in this manner. Because where the process management standard is under direct control of front-line managers and supervisors, and the systems management standard is under direct control of Executive Management, it is most likely that these will be most readily adopted.

The aligned leadership standard appears more difficult. While it could be evaluated by an agency executive officer, it could also be perceived as a career risk since it would be potentially critical of superiors. In this regard, it is supposed that legislative bodies would probably either have to request such an evaluation of themselves and their own management outcome, or else such an evaluation would need to be conducted on their behalf by an independent outside agency.

Voluntary use of the standards provides a means of demonstrating the excellence of operations already achieved and will help identify any areas for improvement. The over-arching benefit of conducting such audits will come from the uniform application of quality science to government, and the uniform implementation of professional standards for measurable value, efficiency, and effectiveness.

The standards make it possible to provide an objective professional opinion of the quality of management of any public entity in a report-card format that will identify the level of quality within each branch and office. It is also an objective and comparative standard that can show which offices or programs may be lagging within any department or agency, and whether the agency or office is making any improvement from year to year. Broad acceptance and use of this standard supports the claim that this standard could transform government.

If adopted as mandatory, the standards will institutionalize and require the use of fundamental and proven practices of quality throughout government. It is expected that their universal implementation will promote a baseline of efficiency and effectiveness in the same manner that requirements for annual financial audits have protected fiscal assets and ensured broad fiscal integrity in the public sector.

The auditable standards have been designed to provide a broad and non-proprietary approach to the use of quality standards in the public sector in a manner that circumvents the need for "white knight" leaders that will adopt or use the latest popular quality practice, whether that is Total Quality Management, Re-Engineering, or Lean/Six Sigma. In fact, the development of standards for each manager and supervisor makes the use of quality practices the responsibility of everyone—not just the latest agency director.* Its emphasis on consistent scorecards also makes it impossible for successive leaders looking for "the next new thing" to abandon the quality practices of predecessors, while they redirect attention to office restructuring, "visioning the future," or any other new initiative. Any loss of efficiency and effectiveness that results will then be obvious. In short, these standards serve to ensure that government entities provide baseline quality, despite the ebb and flow of changes in political leadership. In addition, it is intended that the standards will be revised and updated in the future by a college of professional overseers associated with the aforementioned Center. The auditable standards have been created to last.

---

* It is noted that two of the "seven deadly diseases" of quality consistently listed by W. Edwards Deming were "lack of constancy of purpose" and "mobility of management," both of which are endemic in government at all levels.

A further understanding of the context of quality practice is also help-ful, so that policy makers understand the background and universality of these standards. As noted briefly in Chapter 2, the current practice of qual-ity in business requires documentation of a process that delivers a defined value to customers, documentation of its requirements (or desired perfor-mance metrics), and the use of a variety of structured tools for continuous process improvement.* The steps in analysis and improvement have most recently been articulated as the DMAIC cycle—Define, Measure, Analyze, Improve, Control, as shown in Figure 8.1.

Common generic steps to achieving appropriate process manage-ment are provided in Chapter 4, under the heading "Steps to Continuous Quality Improvement."

Currently popular applications of quality in the private sector include Lean Process Management, Six Sigma, Kaizen, ISO process certifica-tion, and some others—all of which are forms of Continuous Quality Improvement. Since the advent of quality science after 1961,† it has evolved progressively through the works of numerous "quality gurus," authors, and practitioners including W. Edwards Deming, Joseph Juran, Kaoru Ishikawa, and Armand Feigenbaum, among others.

So now we have many books, and many schools of practice, and none have been able to solve the problem of failed implementation and incon-sistent practice. The development of each school has been an attempt by an author or practitioner to put Quality Science and Process Science into "their" formulaic body of knowledge, with clear step-by-step instructions on how to achieve process improvement and what tools to use to do so. It is reminiscent of watching a favorite cooking show, where a series of chefs is each trying to bake the perfect coffee cake. One uses a bit more cinna-mon and the other adds yogurt instead of sour cream. But the end result is pretty close—a coffee cake.

The same is true for our quality science, and all the recipes, done correctly, should get close to the same result, with most of the same ingredients.

---

* Three classic books regarding the methods and tools of continuous process improvement include: (1) *The Team Handbook*, by Peter Scholtes; (2) *The Memory Jogger: A Pocket Guide of Tools for Continuous Improvement*, GOAL/QPC; and (3) *The Deming Management Method* by Mary Walton.

† The year 1961 was picked since it correlates with the date of publication of *Total Quality Control* by Armand Feigenbaum and is proximate to the date that Ichiro Ishikawa joined the University of Tokyo (1960) and introduced the concept of quality circles (1962) in conjunction with the Japanese Union of Scientists and Engineers (JUSE). A variety of significant milestones and publications followed, most notably including Dr. W. Edwards Deming's 1982 book *Out of the Crisis*.

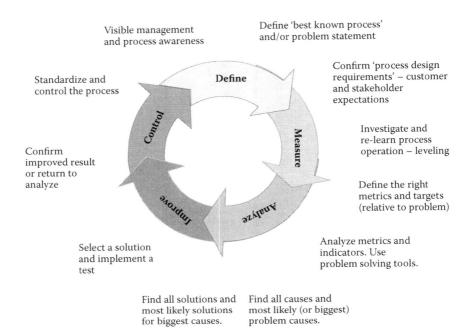

Visible management
and process awareness

Define 'best known process'
and/or problem statement

Standardize and
control the process

Confirm 'process design
requirements' – customer
and stakeholder
expectations

Confirm
improved result
or return to
analyze

Investigate and
re-learn process
operation – leveling

Define the right
metrics and targets
(relative to problem)

Select a solution
and implement a
test

Analyze metrics and
indicators. Use
problem solving tools.

Find all solutions and
most likely solutions
for biggest causes.

Find all causes and
most likely (or biggest)
problem causes.

FIGURE 8.1
DMAIC cycle—Define, Measure, Analyze, Improve, Control.

The primary focus for the current practice of "Lean" in government is a search for waste, or alternately, for clear identification of value-add. The practice of "Six Sigma" provides a focus on performance measurement, and the development of process that will produce with greatest reliability considering those process measures. The practice of "re-engineering" often looks for new technology or methods, and the practice of ISO certification often emphasizes standardization of existing best practice. These methods add tools and methods that can drive process management and continuous improvement, and all are direct withdrawals from the collective body of knowledge of Quality Science.

The desire to name and claim that body of knowledge and to develop uniform practices for its implementation has only one legitimate basis—that it would provide a sound and sustained means of implementation. That has not turned out to be true, especially in the public sector. Except for a few unique tools and specific implementation frameworks, there is nothing fundamentally new or unique that any of the many schools, centers, and consultants have brought. This is true despite the recent ascendancy of the "Lean Six Sigma" framework, which is in fact a consolidation of both Lean

Manufacturing practices that evolved within Toyota Production Systems beginning in the early 1980s and the Six Sigma methods first developed at Motorola Corporation in the mid-1980s—neither of which are particularly good fits for government in any case. Both practices are adaptations of the works of Deming, Juran, Ishikawa, and Feigenbaum, and have only added some redefinitions of terms and goals unique to manufacturing, along with some additional analytic tools. These two frameworks have been refined and popularized through a group of corporations that have successfully used these frameworks since their initial deployment, and then uncomfortably joined as a single discipline. Their application to government requires removal of manufacturing-specific practices such as "one-piece-flow" and are then focused largely on elimination of waste and standardization of process, which are the traditional focus of quality science as a whole.

The term continuous quality improvement (CQI) is a reference to the same fundamentals of quality science on which Lean is built. Some of its key concepts are as follows:

- Process quality depends on understanding and meeting customer (and process design) requirements.
- Quality improvement comes from systematic analysis and improvement of work processes though the use of the scientific method (sometimes called PDCA = "plan/do/check act"). This is also sometimes called "DMAIC."
- Process improvement is based on doing right things right the first time and eliminating waste (sometimes called "prevention").
- The best way to eliminate waste is to redesign processes to prevent error.
- Error prevention depends on creating stable process, with managed variation in output.
- Management's job is to optimize the system by making employees successful and creating a workforce that is empowered and engaged.
- Process management is based on continual tracking of performance measures, that align process outputs and outcomes, and with customer requirements.

The reasons for the continuing desire to adapt and rename quality science are twofold. First, there is a legitimate need to continue to challenge and refresh basic concepts, in part so they can be "sold" to new generations of organizational leaders who are looking for the next new thing.

Second, quality practitioners continue to be concerned about the acknowledged failure of organizations who adapt quality practices to provide demonstrable results, but either do not achieve them or cannot sustain them—called the failure rate. Jerry J. Mairani, a colleague and 2011 Chair of ASQ conducted and led a study of the failure rate of quality initiatives in the private sector and government from 2005 through 2012. He concluded between 50–70% of all quality initiatives fail within three years. Mairani's conclusion was that the primary reasons for the quality initiative failure rate is: (1) lack of leadership, (2) lack of change management, (3) poor execution of the method, and (4) a failure to demonstrate the true financial value of the quality method.

It is clear that new quality frameworks, such as Lean Six Sigma, are first invented as specific tailored adaptations to a particular organization, and then more broadly "sold" to a larger group that is seeking to avoid a "failed implementation." However, a 2010 e-mail from Lean Institute founder Jim Womack to Institute members noted that even Lean has suffered from failure. "Put another way, many of us in the Lean Community have focused our attention on improving core processes in organizations by deploying brilliant tools when we should have been focused on improving the management process itself. That is the fundamental problem." He continued: "We need to acknowledge a simple but awkward fact: The right, Lean management system for each organization can only be discovered through experimentation in the form of PDCA.* And this requires a dialogue in each organization about the value-creating work of management and how to merge it with sustainable process improvement. Indeed, a discussion of how to make continuous improvement a core activity of line management."

The auditable standards, however, make it unlikely that organizations will abandon the proper use of quality management practices in the future, for two reasons. First, the requirements for compliance have been reduced to fundamental and obvious disciplines that are readily audited. Second, the required practices are objectively measured. In this way, the public and legislative leaders can easily take action where standards lapse. Additionally, bond underwriters and insurance brokers can easily incorporate quality audit scores in risk calculations, so there will be

---

* The term PDCA refers to an early description of Continuous Quality Improvement—or Quality Science—popularized by W. Edwards Deming. The acronym, Plan/Do/Check/Act is a different description of the problem-solving logic described within the DMAIC cycle, through Define/Measure/Analyze/Improve/Control.

fiscal implications of quality management. Special masters and receivers appointed by courts in municipal bankruptcy actions would also be well advised to consider audits as a part of recovery plans.

Indeed, if the leadership system requires a minimum standard of compliance, for whatever reason, the possibility of failure—or abandonment—in the use of quality management practices will disappear. There will be no need to "sell" the use of quality practices to leadership teams and so the need to develop clever new consulting packages will also disappear. Any agency that abandons quality management will be quickly identified in future audits, and will suffer the result.

9

Four Necessary Strategies

While this book anticipates broad and immediate change from implementation of auditable quality standards in government, it is also aware of four significant barriers that remain and that should be directly addressed in each adopting jurisdiction to the extent possible. The following strategies are therefore recommended for action.

CREATE AN IMPERATIVE FOR CONSENSUS

The term majority rule, minority rights is fundamental to American democracy, and to other world democracies that are organized as "majoritarian" systems.* This system is sometimes characterized as "winner take all" and, lately, has also been characterized by an unwillingness to adopt any kind of compromise or consensus. This system contrasts with parliamentary consensus democracies that have multiparty systems, and inclusive cabinet coalitions, and which are more likely to reach compromise and consensus as a necessity for everyday operations.

Majoritarian systems in America have created an atmosphere of arena sports, where voters come to the arena primarily to cheer for their team to win, and then often lose interest in further discussion of issues. This dynamic of contention, and win-lose, is inadvertently heralded by the press, which has labeled the states as "red" and "blue," and speculates about which color will control Congress and the State houses. Consensus should not cheer for red and blue, but should instead seek wisdom in their combination. An educated press should be cheering for shades of purple.

---

* The term was created by Arend Lijphard in his 1999 book, *Patterns of Democracy: Government Forms and Performance in 36 Countries.*

Analysis of the "winner take all" statistics in the U.S. presidential elections shows that even when there is a 51% vote for the winner, it represents a clear minority of the over 221 million "voting eligible" persons in the nation*—in many years less than 30%. In other words, 7 out of 10 eligible American voters are often governed by a president that only 3 out of 10 supported. In this kind of an environment, perhaps consensus governance should receive more attention. Instead, the same kind of majoritarian philosophy seems to drive Congress, where representatives are willing to endanger the credit rating and fiscal stability of the public rather than come to fundamental agreement on a balanced budget. The underlying Congressional behavior must be based on a perception that unless my own personal preference is a choice, that I do not have to agree on or accept any other—regardless of national consequences. Perhaps they should remember that if voters had that right, we would not have representatives in Congress!

As noted previously, quality in government can best be achieved through a shared and measurable definition of desired outcomes and through application of scientific method to test the systems and processes that are established to accomplish those outcomes. This requires that individual members are open to change and learning and are not afraid to change course or admit mistake. It requires civil discourse, independence of thought, learning, and analysis, and it requires a culture where changing your mind—based on facts—is not publicly dishonored but, instead, is a mark of positive character.

One key facet to civil discourse that allows for creative solutions and for real learning is that groups must demonstrate collective wisdom. In a book on this subject, James Surowiecki† noted that four key behaviors must be practiced by the elected representatives within government in order for wise solutions to be developed. These include:

- **Diversity of opinions**—Each person or interest in the decision-making group has perspective or knowledge that is at least partially different from others.
- **Independence of positions**—The opinions of decision makers are not influenced to conform to those around them.

---

* Based on 2010 statistics.
† *Wisdom of Crowds* (2004) by James Surowiecki. Doubleday Press.

- **Decentralization**—The group can get local or specialized information in its mix of knowledge and perspective.
- **Aggregation**—A rational mechanism exists for turning private judgments into a collective decision.

Those who know government well will readily admit that independence of positions is probably the fatal flaw in our present system because partisan control of the elective process forces out non-conformity in a number of ways. Particularly, non-conforming members of a political party are often stripped of political power and through diversion of funding to run for re-election, are often forced from office. Because non-conformity is not permitted, a respect for a diversity of opinions is undermined.

At the same time, there is often a lack of good faith among members at the time of discussion or debate. In fact, many observers have noted that the lack of civil discourse is the defining factor of our contemporary government. Stephen Miller, author of the book *Conversation: A History of a Declining Art*, says that Americans and their political leaders are increasingly living in "anger communities." Miller says that anger communities are "preoccupied with their political opponents," and that they can tell you a lot more about what they hate than what they support.

Another observer noted that members of anger communities "tend to talk only to one another, or at least to listen only to one another, fueling and amplifying their outrage."* So, participants in anger communities welcome advocacy news shows and talk radio, where shouting and insults about their "stupid opposition" is a primary goal.

It would seem that a large share of the voting public has knowingly or unwittingly gotten sucked into a nonproductive anger vortex, in which the constructive discussion of issues and opportunities are not a part. In 2004, a New York Times bestselling book was written entitled, *Don't Think of an Elephant*. It was a guidebook for politicians on how to "frame" their comments in simplistic terms and buzz words meant to sway the public. The author, of course, was not openly in favor of dumbing down political discourse, but thought that his favored political party was being minimized by the opposition, and that it was time to fight fire with fire.

Wedge politics build on the idea of anger communities and is a partisan strategy that has been openly talked about for at least 15 years, and which attempts to find a divisive or controversial social or political issue that

---

* Cass Sunstein, *Why Societies Need Dissent* (2003), as cited by Stephen Miller.

splits apart or creates a "wedge" in the support base of the opposing political group. Wedge issues are then focused on in a political campaign in an attempt to weaken the unity of the other group or to entice voters in the divided group to give their support to the initiating group.

The overriding concern with maintaining political sound bites that appeal to each politician's "anger communities" also negates the ability to consider independent information sources, which is the third factor on the above-stated list of attributes of collective wisdom. In the current partisan environment, information that does not conform to existing opinions is often rejected. "Global warming" is a case in point.

Given the history and apparent strength of the commitment to these majoritarian systems, the hope for creating an imperative for consensus seems difficult and may ultimately hinge on reducing the power of bipartisan political democracy. This could include removing the power of political parties to exclusively control who will run for office, and their power to punish representatives or candidates who deviate from official party positions. Perhaps it should limit their power to consolidate special interest group money, or to operate tax-free. Other options may be to charge elected representatives who vote the "party line" and fail to reach compromise with official malfeasance—and abdication of duty. In the future, it may ultimately be possible to adopt new methods of direct-democracy to replace partisan-representative government. These are certainly long-term options.

More actionable in the near term are the following. We can:

- Require each legislative body to vote on consensus objectives and a performance scorecard, and where they will not commission an independent third-party organization to do so.
- Establish pay for performance for elected representatives.

END INCENTIVES FOR BUILDING BUREAUCRACY

It is a little recognized fact that in almost every government jurisdiction everywhere, there are distinct incentives for building the size of the bureaucracy and distinct threats for supporting reductions. This has created a kind of "cone of silence" within the professional civil service, in which elected representatives and others seeking to "find the fat" in government cannot do so. Those who know where it is have no incentive to reveal it and hidden motives for keeping it concealed.

The natural tendency of government to grow was first pointed out in 1957 by a man named C. Northcoat Parkinson, who was a British civil servant in Singapore, and who himself named it the "law of the rising pyramid." Parkinson concluded that government agencies, once established, have an intrinsic force of growth. He explained this growth because of civil servants who obtain greater pay and status primarily as a result of increases in the size of their staff. In other words, those who can justify more staff get a promotion while those that achieve economies and reduce the need for staff are penalized.

One of his specific observations follows: "Supervisors naturally want to hire staff to assist in supervision. There is a natural incentive to increase the amount of staff, because manager pay is determined by the numbers of subordinates. If you get a new project and have a solid need to increase a work unit from three to five employees, and then one year later decide you could improve the work—do you tell anyone? No."

In support of this conclusion, Parkinson studied the British Admiralty in the period from 1914 to 1928, when the commissioned capital ships had decreased from 62 to 20, and the numbers of officers and crew had decreased by 31.5%, the number of Admiralty officials (headquarters administrative staff) had almost doubled, from 2000 to 3569. He also studied the Colonial Office from 1935 to 1954, and found the same kind of growth, even though the territory and population administered by the Colonial Office had shrunk dramatically after 1947, as successive British colonies achieved independence. In fact, the Colonial Office in 1954 employed 1661 civil servants, while it had had just 372 in 1935. Parkinson concluded: "The fact is that the number of officials and the quantity of the work are not related to each other at all."

He explained that the work of any government agency "swells in importance and complexity in a direct ratio with the time to be spent." Parkinson said that two motive factors cause that growth: First, that managers obtain increased pay and status when they multiply subordinates and restrict the number of professional peers. Second, he concluded that officials can be rewarded rather than penalized when they make work for each other. Neither Parkinson nor any government professional argues that civil servants deliberately hire persons when there is nothing for them to do. However, it is clear that the conventional wisdom in civil service is to develop staffing that is capable of fully addressing a complex body of work whenever possible, rather than to "bet" on an intrinsic ability to reduce the complexity of work.

The author's work in government consulting and civil service classification analysis has independently seen Parkinson's law at work many times. All current contemporary civil service pay systems use job classification standards as a method of determination of classification, and thus pay levels. It is a universal truth that every employee everywhere is strongly motivated toward advancement and pay increase, and is thus highly focused on what their agency's specific classification standards might provide. What they do offer any intelligent reader is a series of classification and complexity standards that consistently reward those with more employees, more programs, and a larger budget. Conversely, persons who once managed larger offices and now manage smaller offices are deemed "working out of class," and are at risk of having to be reduced in pay. This is hardly an environment in which mangers can be expected to come forward with ideas on savings and program reduction!

The reason that the pockets and veins of fat in government are never discovered is because they are hidden from outsiders and ignored by insiders because of a fear that cuts will hurt the income or job status of those who know too well where they are. The two barriers are fairly simple:

1. The fear of workers who reveal them that they will be laid off and unemployed because of the act;
2. The fear of supervisors and managers that if the size of their workforce is diminished, or the number of program offices reduced, that their own management job classification will be diminished and their positions will be downgraded.

Parenthetically, it might be noted that a third important source of "fat" in government is the failure of elected representatives to prioritize the work requirement, which will be addressed through the aligned leadership objectives standard. However, when that is done it will be necessary for elected leaders to be able to cooperate with front-line managers, both in terms of the restructuring of work as well as obtaining ideas from those front-line managers on the simplification of work requirements for existing work processes deemed critical.

BUILD A SAFETY NET FOR CHAMPIONS OF EFFICIENCY

One of the most significant barriers to implementation of savings and efficiency in government comes from the unrecognized and justified fear of government workers that pointing out efficiencies could cost them their job. While it seems counterintuitive to elected officials and to the public, there is a need to guarantee the jobs of those with the courage to come forward with improvement.

A 2016 study conducted by the ASQ Government Division* found that 27.3% of the team leaders who conducted structured process improvement projects said there was a concern regarding a possible reduction of jobs from those improvement activities, and most of those felt this concern had either a large or moderate impact on team recommendations. Consultants to process improvement teams such as the author have had face-to-face discussions with many government process improvement team members and have seen more than a few teams entirely back away from improvements due to the fear of job loss.

Both elected officials and the public need to acknowledge that there should be a reward offered for those willing to pioneer improvement efforts that have the potential to streamline government and provide efficiency and savings. The reward that is necessary is a guarantee that anyone who is willing to bring such savings forward should either be assured they will get a similar job somewhere else in government or a promotion! If officials do nothing, we will maintain the current fear of coming forward with ideas for savings, and due to a loss of jobs.

Of course, the common retort to this argument is, "How will we ever streamline government if we promise jobs to everyone who identifies a lack of efficiency?" The answer is patience—and not really for very long. If we use our "displaced" workers to fill vacancies created by the normal annual retirements, promotions, and transfers, we can be assured that we could accommodate up to a 10% staff reduction (if desired) through normal attrition. The challenge of our governments then is to have the courage to guarantee jobs, even though it may draw pubic concern.

The issue regarding job loss was described as the principle of driving out fear by W. Edwards Deming and noted by many of the pioneers of

* The study was conducted between July and September 2016, and surveyed the results of 79 Lean process teams throughout North American, at the federal, state, and local level. Results are available in the government division library, at www.asq.org/gov, under Quality Information/Library.

the "total quality management" effort in the decades from 1980–1990. It recognizes that you cannot get employees to actively participate in the improvement of work processes when it might cost them their jobs.

An important part of this change will require that elected leaders abandon their usual adversarial stance and "fighting the establishment," and be partners in protecting government workers from catastrophic career impacts. It is often observed among the professional civil service that elected representatives love to "grandstand" for the press by pointing to some real or perceived agency inefficiency. This stance may be a form of the earlier cited "anger communities" that makes elected representatives appear to be "fighting" to get fiscal responsibility "against" hopelessly irresponsible civil servants. In fact, it is just perceived adversarial atmosphere that motivates civil servants to hide temporary or occasional situations of overstaffing in case of future cutbacks. The expected adversarial relationship creates a game of hide and seek in the first place.

So, at the very least, it will be necessary for a moratorium on one-upmanship regarding agencies that are willing to publicly admit to any inefficiencies. When continuous quality improvement is launched in such an agency, elected representatives will need to provide a guarantee that no one in these agencies will lose a job for one year or more, or they may get a job in another agency. This is the only way that employees at all levels in the subject agency will feel the security necessary to restructure work and achieve performance efficiencies. While offering such a pledge might seem counterintuitive, it must be remembered that these savings will not happen at all without it. In addition, every organization that has ever achieved significant voluntary restructuring has had to follow this route.

As with the strategy of creating an imperative for consensus, the actions described above are likely to be long term. A short-term and more pragmatic immediate concept would be to establish a separate Department of Transition Management or Project Management. This office could institutionalize the promise of a legislature not to harm any employee or group of employees that come forward with cost-savings ideas and would provide a job at the same pay rate* for any such employee for up to two years. Such an office could be assigned to carry out any or all the short-term projects of government, of which there are many. Transitioning

---

* Since significant and continuing savings would be associated with any transition of this kind, a progressive legislature might even want to add a 50% one-time salary bonus to such employees.

employees could use the two-year hiatus to seek jobs in other branches of government.

One last impediment to such transitions is the specificity of management job classifications, which sometimes require such a high level of specific program knowledge that such a manager might be unlikely to find similarly paid work in another department. So, for example, if I am the senior manager in a telecommunications office that inspects FAX machines, and those machines are becoming obsolete, I may not want to report that obsolescence, even with the safety net of a Department of Transitions.

A strategy to address that fear would be to characterize all management positions as "Project Managers" and to regard all assigned programs as projects of one or more year's duration. Then I would have a natural incentive to bid for more programs—more work—to support my job classification. I could also give up or substitute programs, or transition to new departments more easily.

MAKE ELECTED REPRESENTATIVES ACCOUNTABLE FOR RESULTS

An unfortunate by-product of our democracy is that elected representatives are not directly held accountable for results achieved by government, and are therefore more focused on criticism. They tend to focus on criticism because it gains headlines and public attention, which creates the perception that they are "doing something." The other category of action that creates the perception of "doing something" is sponsoring legislation or getting legislation enacted.

Legislative action, however, is often most difficult on the large and substantive issues of the day, and so the legislation most easily passed is for a "pet project" or minor grievance that often either spends money or requires agencies to expand the scope of their services, or to add a new program. Thus, so much legislation adds to the complexity and cost of our government as it now exists, rather than creating simplification or streamlining.

Overall, even though elected representatives are conceptually viewed as being similar to a corporation board of directors, in reality they are different. This is because they do not have a vested interest in the better performance of government, and are not held accountable for showing this kind of result. This is in large part because the public cannot now see the value of their legislature nor see whether any efficiency or effectiveness resulted from its actions.

This is where the importance of the aligned leadership objective standard comes in because it provides a way to see that value, and to promote this kind of positive change. The aligned leadership objective then could become the capstone to achieving best value, efficiency, and effectiveness in government. Because it is hard to imagine any kind of fundamental shift in achieving results from government without an impartial results scorecard, the following ideas are all based on adoption of this standard. Without that change there are few good options and certainly no easy ones.

In the first edition of this book, it was recommended that pay for performance may be one way to focus elected representatives on results, and that perhaps setting legislative and executive salaries on a sliding scale based on achieved results would work. If such a principle could be adopted, it could be supported by the maturity score achieved in the aligned leadership objective standard.

Another thought is that legislators could be subjected to shorter term limits if they do not create consensus goals and a scorecard, as is recommended by the new leadership standard. Alternately, term limits would be removed if they achieved the highest-level rankings on the standard.

A final thought is that the aligned leadership objectives as applied to the set of agencies overseen by any group of legislators, perhaps through committee assignments, could also build interest in results. This might require a realignment of the committee structures so that each specific committee on which a representative sits provides oversight for a specific department—even if it also has more generalized duties. In this way, a specific group of elected representatives would be held accountable for the results of each department, including the accomplishment of its assigned goals and the resultant evaluation of its programs. This would be a form of putting authority and accountability in the same place, which is a rule of good management.

Any of these ideas will of course require tailoring and adoption by our legislatures and government executives and should be supported by an independent assessment of compliance with the aligned leadership objective. This in turn may require either an independent audit agency be given this authority, perhaps under an independent elected office. Regardless, the concept should work and is itself offered as a best possible management practice.

10

Supportive Culture and Values

The culture and values within any organization, or solely within its leadership group, can be a tremendous driving force for change, or conversely, a totally suffocating inhibitor. A suffocating cultural fear can prevent any kind of action, even if it is necessary to overcome something obviously wrong or unfair. The fear of a ruling party is the sole reason that Nelson Mandela was incarcerated for 27 years in a South African prison for advocating the right to vote by all people—even though that same right had been historically proven around the world. In a still-significant but much smaller way, this author has seen more than one quality effort die a sudden death because a new leader viewed it unimportant or a waste of time.

So, while implementation of auditable quality standards depends on an organizational culture (or an electorate) that will support and reward its use, it also recognizes that its impact will either be accelerated or inhibited based on the existence of several cultural values, and this chapter will highlight those as final guidance on developing value, efficiency, and effectiveness in government.

At least three of these foundational values are full chapters in this author's previous book, *Management Strategy: Creating Excellent Organizations.** Those values are

- A partnership between front line and leadership
- Teaching leaders to listen
- The right to ask questions

---

* Mallory, Richard. (2002). *Management Strategy: Creating Excellent Organizations.* Trafford Publishing. Available at http://bookstore.trafford.com/Products/SKU-000147416/Management -Strategy.aspx.

Consistent with these values the fundamental practice of quality science is fact-based management and relies on the collective wisdom of each organization and leadership system to target, evaluate, and deliver high-quality products and services. These are sometimes also referred to as the values of empowerment, engagement, and participation.

The Core Values and Concepts of the Criteria for Performance Excellence* calls this "Valuing Workforce Members and Partners," and says: "An organization's success depends … on a safe, trusting and cooperative environment." It notes that "major changes in valuing your workforce members include: (1) demonstrating your leaders' commitment to their success; (2) providing motivation and recognition that go beyond the regular compensation system; (3) offering development and progression within your organization; (4) sharing your organization's knowledge so your workforce can better serve your customers and contribute to achieving your strategic objectives; (5) creating an environment that encourages intelligent risk taking to achieving innovation, and (6) creating a supportive environment for a diverse workforce."

Some very simple ground rules for the direction of values in organizations might therefore include:

- **No eagles:** Meaning when employee and management groups get together to talk about areas for improvement or change, there is no "rank." Everyone has an equal right to ask questions and to be heard, and all decisions are based on their own facts and merit.
- **No one left behind:** Meaning that the change effort should not favor any unit or program at the expense of others. The focus of all effort is on a better system, and better value for external customers and stakeholders. There should be no losers inside the organization. "The aim of a system is to make everyone a winner."
- **Cooperation:** Meaning that new partnerships will be necessary, between units within the organization, between departments and levels of government, and between elected officials and work units deep in the organization. If simplification of law or regulations will make work easier, legislators should look at that as potentially more important than any as new legislation. More than ever government must work together as a system for the greater public good.

---

* Criteria for Performance Excellence (2013–2014), Baldrige Performance Excellence Program, p. 38. www.nist.gov/baldrige.

- **No fear:** All parties should feel free to ask questions or try new things without fear of retaliation or career harm. All parties engaged in change must seek to encourage and sustain the others.
- **Future vision:** A focus on long-term and future needs must be a routine part of governance. Whenever possible, government and its requirements must be liberated from the past.

While the need for a positive culture and values are supportive of change, they are the most difficult to include in auditable standards, and have therefore been excluded. Jurisdictions may wish to explore a companion strategy that touches on some of these values through an employee or organizational climate survey. This is encouraged.

The use of auditable quality standards is therefore presented to the world, with the anticipation that at long last, the voice of the customer will engage and empower government and make it an able partner for our future prosperity.

Appendix A: System Management Standard

Purpose and Structure of a System	Goal Directedness through Measures and Feedback	Management of Intervening Variables and Risk	Alignment, Evaluation, and Improvement
0 – The system is named and has known purpose, but no structure. Specific system actions, events, and activities respond to outside influences and may be based on political agendas or individual judgements, without regard to analysis or past learning experience.	0 – The system has no clearly defined outcomes, and no expectations for its performance. Its hoped-for outcomes are ambiguous.	0 – Intervening variables and risk have not been identified or are unknown.	0 – There are no systematic efforts to learn and improve. The resources and personnel that constitute the system do not recognize its existence.
1 – The system has some documentation but is not mapped. There is some recognition of the system cycle with some of the principal activity groups[a] recognized or documented and mapped.	1 – The existence and use of currently defined systems can be linked to some objective and positive organizational performance.	1 – The principal intervening variables[b] in the system cycle have been identified, and response scenarios are known.	1 – Some documented history of systems evaluation and change. Major system risks have been mapped. Resources and personnel who contribute are informed of the system and its purpose.

(Continued)

Purpose and Structure of a System	Goal Directedness through Measures and Feedback	Management of Intervening Variables and Risk	Alignment, Evaluation, and Improvement
2 – The system is defined and documented at the high level and mapped. The system map includes all principal activity groups and some of its specific contributing tasks and activities. Output requirements exist for the system as a whole.	2 – There is some structured feedback on system performance that is based on documented system output requirements, and to its defined purpose. Much of feedback may be subjective or milestone related. Output requirements can be shown to be linked to requirements of system stakeholders and customers. There are no output requirements specific to each principal activity group.	2 – Intervening variables have been identified for all principal activity groups, and response scenarios documented. The organization conducts at least annual risk analysis, and has documented responses to principal risks.	2 – System leadership is connected to the resources and personnel, and they are aware of its approach, structure (map), and their role in delivery of contributing tasks and activities. Accountability and responsibility for actions within each principal activity group is known. The system of deployment is linked to management activity.

(Continued)

Purpose and Structure of a System	Goal Directedness through Measures and Feedback	Management of Intervening Variables and Risk	Alignment, Evaluation, and Improvement
3 – The system has a defined approach and a planned deployment. There is a pattern and purpose specific to each principal activity group. The map has been in place for at least one year, and is used for management analysis and planning. Tasks, activities, and contributing factors have been developed for some but not all of the principal activity groups. Requirements exist for the system as a whole and for several subcomponents. Leadership has some evidence that the system operates as designed, using indicators and other performance measures.	3 – Executive managers regularly receive and review performance feedback, including subjective feedback and objective performance measures. This performance feedback is specific to the system as a whole and to many of its principal activity groups. Performance feedback includes indicators regarding timely completion of milestones and quality of delivery of defined requirements. There is some definition of subordinate process interface, with defined requirements for system inputs and process outputs. There are defined requirements for these system inputs and outputs, and feedback systems exist to capture relative performance in these areas. Performance feedback, taken as a whole, shows a satisfactory level of performance in all areas and some improvement in key areas.	3 – Contingency plans for principal intervening systems variables have been documented and deployed, at least in some instances. An annual system risk identification review is conducted, and results are documented. Root cause analysis is performed to analyze risks. Other possible tools include business environment analysis, SWOT, technical, hazard and failure assessment. Risk is analyzed in terms of likelihood, consequence and timeframe.	3 – The designated system undergoes annual evaluation, improvement, and change, and all its contributing and participating personnel are at least informed and consulted. Specific responsibilities and accountabilities[d] for each principal activity group have been defined. Organizational learning through operations of the system are showing successive refinements and change in performance and management. Feedback, and in risk identification and management.

(Continued)

Purpose and Structure of a System	Goal Directedness through Measures and Feedback	Management of Intervening Variables and Risk	Alignment, Evaluation, and Improvement
4 – Leadership has mapped and documented the system covering all tasks, accountabilities, and contributing factors. Major intervening variables and system risks have been identified. There is a comprehensive system map that shows all activity groups, demonstrates order, pattern, and purpose. Milestones are known and tracked for the identified system delivery cycle. Deployment is specific to the means used to manage the system and to ensure its continuing operations according to design. Leadership has indicators and other performance measures in place for all principal activity groups. There is evidence of the use of this system management structure for two or more years.	4 – Objective and measurable feedback/results are linked to this organizational system, covering all tasks, accountabilities, and contributing factors, and to system inputs from subordinate processes and to process outputs from the system. There are demonstrated positive levels of performance in many or most measured areas.	4 – Both risk analysis and risk management planning are used, and there is documented evidence of implementation of risk management. Root cause analysis and other tools are used to design risk management plans, and to identify and manage risks.	4 – There is annual analysis of system effectiveness and development of lessons learned. Update and change is considered annually, both in systems operations and in the risk management plan. Responsibilities, accountability, consultation, and informing roles have been identified for each primary activity group and for dependent tasks and activities.

(Continued)

Purpose and Structure of a System	Goal Directedness through Measures and Feedback	Management of Intervening Variables and Risk	Alignment, Evaluation, and Improvement
5 – There is documented evidence of an ordered system that delivers uniform and predictable quality outputs over multiple operational cycles. The ordered system is supported by a system map and supporting documents covering all tasks, accountabilities, and contributing factors. Major intervening variables and system risks have been identified. The system map links to process maps as necessary, to accomplish organizational goals, and requirements statements for process inputs or outputs are built into systems requirements.	5 – Performance feedback and objective measures are linked to this system and all its defined activity groups. Positive levels and trends exist for the entire system and for all its principal activities. Several indicators and measures are available for each defined activity group. There is evidence that the performance of this defined system has improved and contributed to improving organizational outcomes over 3 or more years.	5 – Risks are actively managed by the risk manager and the risk owner, and progress is reported to management on a regular basis. System design and structure have been modified to lessen the impact or occurrence of intervening variable and risks. There is documented evidence of the use of analysis to lessen risk and system impacts. There is documented evidence of systems learning and improvement. There is evidence of systematic risk identification, tracking, analysis and controls, or mitigations in place.	5 – There is evidence of continuous systematic annual improvement, participated in by all defined systems personnel. There are measurable, positive results on outcomes, and in each activity group, with demonstrated positive relationship to all dependent processes.

(Continued)

Purpose and Structure of a System	Goal Directedness through Measures and Feedback	Management of Intervening Variables and Risk	Alignment, Evaluation, and Improvement
System deployment is specific to the means used to manage the system and to ensure its continuing operations according to design. Operational deployment is supported by responsibilities and accountability for each contributing resource group, and through the use of indicators and performance measures for all principal activity groups. There is evidence of the use of this system management structure for 3 or more years.			

[a] Principal activity groups are generally represented at the highest level by milestones and check gates. At the next lower level, they show the tasks, activities, and contributing factors that create its valuable outputs.

[b] Intervening variables are the categorical variables in system cycles that require adjustments to the known and expected pattern of performance—they are akin to common cause variation in processes.

[c] As in project management, the principal activity groups of a system will benefit using a RACI (Responsible, Accountable, Consulted, Informed) matrix, that ensures the progressive completion of successive dependent tasks.

[d] The responsibilities and accountabilities for each principal activity group consist of linkage to organizational positions or groups. They ensure that personnel know roles and accountability during the value creation cycle of each system step.

Index

Page numbers followed by f, t, and n indicate figures, tables, and notes, respectively.